THE COMPLETE GUIDE TO FISHING SKILLS

FISHING SKILLS

THE COMPLETE GUIDE TO
FISHING
SKILLS

TONY WHIELDON

WARD LOCK

First published in Great Britain in 1988
by Ward Lock, Villiers House, 41/47 Strand
London WC2N 5JE England.

A Cassell imprint

Reprinted 1991

Printed and bound in England by Clays Ltd, St Ives plc.

British Library Cataloguing in Publication Data

The Complete guide to fishing skills.
  Angling – Manuals
  799.1'2

  ISBN 1 85079 187 2

Contents

Introduction

During the period of producing the little books, some of which make up this volume, I have attempted to retain the theme of simplicity. Uncluttered, thoughtfully selected tackle plus a knowledge of the water being fished are, in my estimation, the two main ingredients which produce success.

It is all too easy, nowadays, for a newcomer to the sport to be confused by the vast selection of tackle, and many fall into the trap of buying equipment without giving it proper thought – adverts in the press for hardly-used tackle are testimony to this.

Venues on the doorstep are often overlooked for what appear to be greener pastures further afield. Give the home waters a fair chance; walk by them, study them in all conditions, get to know them intimately and they will all yield their treasures. One of the biggest thrills in angling is to find a new water and explore it with the rod. This does not necessarily mean travelling great distances – look at an Ordnance Survey map of your area and pinpoint areas of water and watercourses. The next step is to obtain permission from the landowner on whose land the lake lies or through which the river runs. Of course, the relevant water authority rod licence will be required even when permission from the landowner has been obtained.

Most of my fishing is done on waters within a twenty-mile radius of my home town of Crediton in Devonshire, and although I would love to fish such great waters as the Tonagariro River in New Zealand, the steelhead rivers of North America or the tigerfish haunts of South Africa, it is doubtful whether my modest little fisheries would lose any of their charm as a result.

Home waters will always be precious to me – so many golden memories of early experiences can never be erased. Wild memories where the elements are remembered more than the actual process of fishing: walking under leaden grey cloud bases as they race over meadows; sheltering in a cow shed during a thunderstorm; painfully pushing through dense blackthorn bushes and brambles to reach a good fishing position: following a stream through woodland smelling of wild garlic, where the pods lie dark and mysterious; walking the long miles home through the dusk, hands scratched and bloody, and dog tired, only to repeat the whole performance the next day.

I always enjoy watching a young angler catching his first fish which hopefully is not too large; for then there is no further goal, no mystery to keep the spark of imagination glowing.

Many of my early golden memories are of completely fishless days, where incidents prompted by my efforts to catch fish remain vividly in my mind's eye. The most enduring image was, paradoxically, the briefest. I was crouching beneath an alder tree on the banks of the River Yeo near Crediton, waiting for a trout to rise again so that I could pin-point his position, when a kingfisher came flashing downstream and perched on the end of the rod, which I was holding horizontally over the water. The rod trembled as the bird retained its balance for a few seconds, then, like a blue arrow, it was away again downstream. There are no colours in nature which match those of the European kingfisher, and the thrill of seeing them at such close quarters has left an indelible image in my mind. On another occasion a fox came to drink immediately opposite my fishing position on a stream which was no more than ten feet wide.

Anglers, be they beginners or experienced fishermen, should be custodians of the waterside. A good angler will leave no evidence of his activities after he has vacated his fishing position. A few flattened blades of grass are obviously unavoidable, but there is no excuse whatsoever for litter, especially discarded nylon line.

I like to think that most anglers are caring, intelligent individuals, but alas the hooligan element exists in angling (coarse, sea and game) as it does in other walks of life. Absolute supervision by bailiffs and wardens is impossible, and it behoves every angler who values the future of our waterside to take any necessary action against the thoughtless few.

Pollution is, of course, the biggest menace and although much has been done to improve some waters and more stringent measures employed to punish the culpable, there is still much to be done. Here again, the angler can play his part by reporting any suspected case of pollution immediately to the nearest water authority representative.

Rivers are the arteries of the land, and they must run clean through the land. The voice of angling (mainly through that clear-eyed movement, the Anglers Cooperative Association) has been instrumental in slowing the acceleration of pollution. Every angler should join the ACA in its fight against pollution. Details can be obtained by writing to:
Anglers Cooperative Association,
23 Castlegate,
Grantham,
Lincs NG31 6SW.
Telephone Grantham: 601008

Let us hope that forward-thinking governments of the present and future will put the matter of river conservation very high on their list of priorities; and that the kingfisher continue to fly.

And the pleasant water-courses,
You could trace them through the valley,
By the rushing in the Spring time,
By the alders in the Summer,
By the white fog in the Autumn,
By the black line in the Winter.

(Henry Wordsworth Longfellow,
Introduction to *Hiawatha*)

Tony Whieldon
Devon
1988

COARSE FISHING

Introduction

The 1980 National Angling Survey revealed that there are more than three million anglers in Britain, over two million of whom are coarse anglers, making it the largest participant sport in the country.

The same survey also revealed that it is a fast-growing sport which every year attracts a great many newcomers – it is for these would-be anglers that this book has been written.

There is a tendency to think of beginners as youngsters – and while that is usually true, it is not inevitably so. I've known men who held their first fishing rods on reaching retirement age! That is one of the marvellous things about angling – you can enjoy it and be successful whatever your age.

On becoming an angler you gain membership of a special 'brotherhood' (or 'sisterhood', for let us not forget that although it's a male-dominated sport, girls and women can and do become excellent anglers); and the essence of this brotherhood is friendliness. I know of no other sport or pastime in which its participants are so ready to help newcomers.

So how does the aspiring coarse angler make a start? First of all, you must acquire the necessary tackle. In this book you'll find some very sound advice on this particular subject, and I recommend that you pay careful heed to it because ill-chosen tackle will prove to be a serious handicap as well as being a waste of money.

Having obtained your new rod, reel and essential accessories you'll doubtless be anxious to start fishing, which is when you'll realize that you cannot just tackle-up beside your nearest lake or river because virtually every water you'll come across will display 'Private' or 'No Fishing' signs.

Obviously, therefore, it's necessary to know something about the way coarse fishing is organized in this country.

Most waters are controlled by angling clubs which can be joined by paying an annual subscription. Once you become a member you will have unlimited fishing in that club's or society's waters for the whole season. That represents very good value when you consider that the average adult fee will range from £5 to £15 per year; in addition, most clubs offer reduced rates for juniors and pensioners.

You can find out the names and addresses of local club secretaries from your tackle-dealer – alternatively a list may be kept by your nearest public library.

Your tackle-dealer will also be able to tell you if there are any day-ticket waters in your area. These can be fished by anyone who buys the necessary permit. Sometimes the permits have to be obtained beforehand (if such is the case your tackle-dealer will probably sell them), but more usual is the system whereby a water-bailiff collects the money and issues you with your ticket while you are fishing. The cost of day-tickets varies, but 50p to £1 would be about average.

Before fishing either club or day-ticket waters, there is an essential and legal requirement to fulfill – you need to obtain a Water Authority rod licence for your area. These, too, can be bought from your tackle-dealer. An adult's licence will probably cost from £3 to £5, and most authorities have special concessionary rates for juniors.

Make sure you get an annual licence that will cover you for the whole of the coarse fishing season (which in most areas runs from 16 June to 14 March inclusive). Short-term licences are only of use to holidaymakers who don't expect to remain in an area for more than a week or two.

Your coarse fish licence does not, incidentally, enable you to fish for salmon or trout – they are classed as game fish and a different (and more expensive) licence is required.

With your licence and your club-card or day-ticket you are now ready to go fishing. But before you rush eagerly down to your chosen water, I would like to offer you an important piece of advice. Please remember at all times that fish are wild creatures; they are timid and easily frightened, so try to avoid heavy footfalls or sudden movements. Think of yourself as a hunter and think of the fish as a cautious quarry that needs to be stalked, outwitted and tempted.

The non-fishing general public cherish the belief that angling success is largely attributable to luck – when they enquire if you've caught anything, the question is usually phrased, 'Had any luck?'. Experienced anglers know that luck plays little or no part in success – oh yes, anyone can get 'once in a lifetime' lucky and catch a solitary big fish, or make an isolated good catch – but consistent success is only achieved through skill and knowledge.

By deciding to read about fishing you have taken the first step towards being a successful angler because you've demonstrated that you want to learn. The best way to learn is under the tutelage of an experienced and expert mentor; so those youngsters who learn about the sport from a fishing father or friend are very fortunate – but for those who don't have that advantage the next best way is to read about it.

Many beginners' guides have been written; some have been very good and a few have been excellent, but none have managed to cram so much valuable information between their covers as has this particular volume. It has often been said that a picture can say more than a thousand words – and there's no doubt that angling lends itself particularly well to the pictorial approach, especially when the drawings are of the calibre of those in this book.

Of all the beginners' guides I've seen, this is the one I would most like to have had available when I first took up fishing as a boy.

Jim Gibbinson,
Cuxton, Kent.

Float rod

Manufactured in fibreglass or carbon fibre — the latter being more expensive but having the advantage of being very light in weight. For the beginner, fibreglass is obviously the practical choice, between 10ft (3·05m.) and 13ft (3·95m) in length. Choose a length to suit your physique.

The complete rod is usually made up of three equal-length sections.

Rings

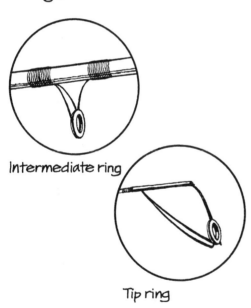

Intermediate ring

Tip ring

Rings are made from chromed steel, stainless steel, aluminium oxide and silicon carbide, which is very expensive, but, being friction free, produces better casting performance as well as prolonging the life span of your line.

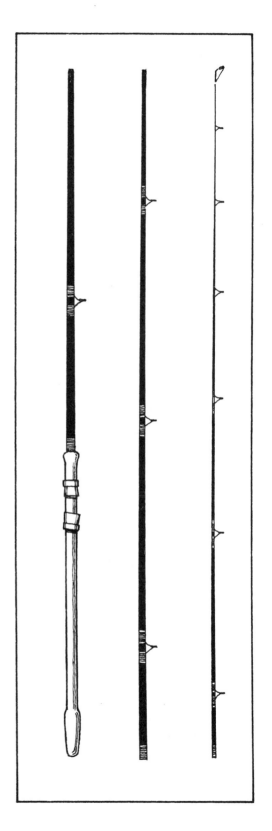

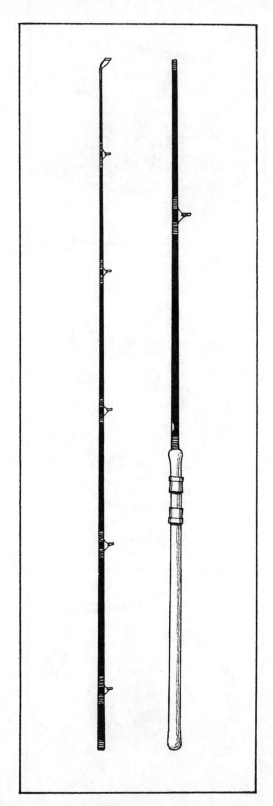

Leger rod

Ranging in length from 9ft (2·75m) to 11ft (3·35m), leger rods are usually made up of two sections. Some have a special screw fitting built into the tip ring to accommodate a swing-tip or a quivertip. Special quiver-tip rods, with the quivertip built into the rod as a permanent fixture, are also available.

Spigot joint

Reverse glass to glass joint

Swing/quivertip fitting

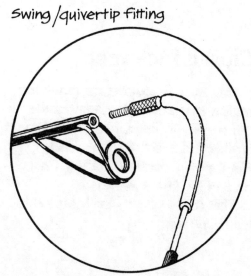

Fixed-spool reel

By far the most popular reel in use in coarse fishing today. When it is correctly loaded with line the static spool allows extremely long casts to be made. An adjustable slipping clutch mechanism can be set to suit the breaking strain of the line, thus making it virtually impossible for a fish to break the line in snag-free water.

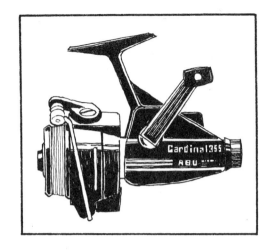

Centrepin reel

In the hands of an expert this is the ideal tool for trotting a float on fast, strong-flowing rivers like the Trent or the Avon. Very fast recovery of line can be achieved by batting the rim of the drum with the hand.

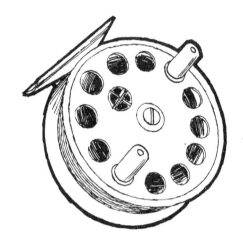

Closed face reel

This is a favourite of many top match anglers, superseding the centrepin in its application when trotting a float downstream. Finger-tip control allows fast and efficient fishing.

This reel is also ideally suited to light-line spinning.

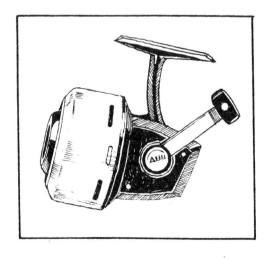

Loading a fixed-spool reel

It is most important to load a fixed-spool reel with the correct amount of line. An incorrectly loaded reel will drastically reduce the distance that a small bait should be cast.

Open the bale arm and secure the end of the line to the spool using a double slip knot.

Face the spool towards the reel, and under gentle pressure wind the line on to the reel spool.

The reel is adequately loaded when the line level is about 1mm under the leading rim of the spool.

Have someone holding the line spool and line as you wind the line on to the reel spool.

Pull knot tight before winding.

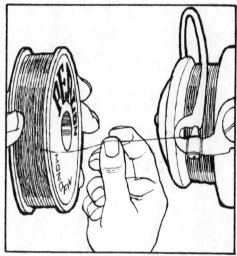

Fine line spool   Heavy line spool

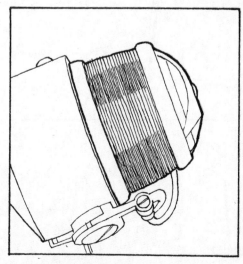

A correctly loaded fixed-spool.

Hooks

Two types of hooks are used in coarse angling – spade-end and eyed. Eyed hooks can be of the flat variety or down-eyed. Spade-end hooks can be purchased already tied to nylon, but many anglers prefer to tie on their own.

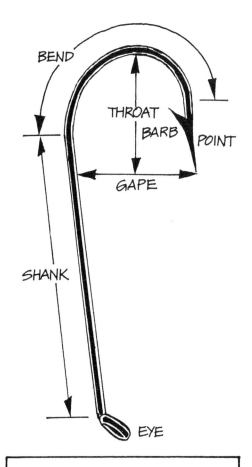

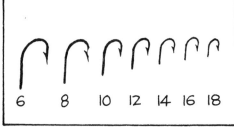

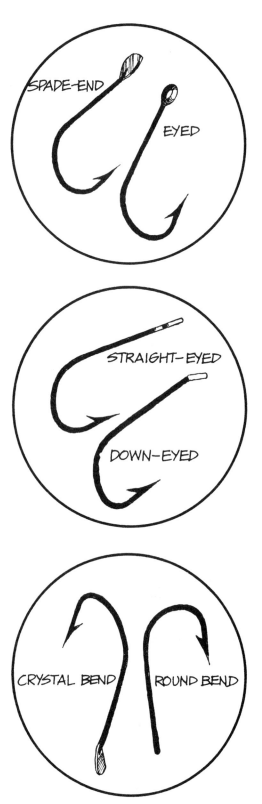

Leads

The Arlesey bomb is, without a doubt, the most popular leger weight. Many anglers use it to the exclusion of all else. A range of Arlesey bombs from ⅛ oz (3g) to 1oz (30g) should meet all your requirements.

The other weights have their uses of course. For example, the drilled bullet is ideal for rolling a bait downstream, whereas the coffin lead has the opposite effect, and anchors the bait.

Barrel leads and jardine spirals are useful for pike fishing, and the ollivette is used with a continental pole.

The plummet is indispensable for finding the depth.

Non-toxic split shot in various sizes is a must in every coarse fisherman's tackle box.

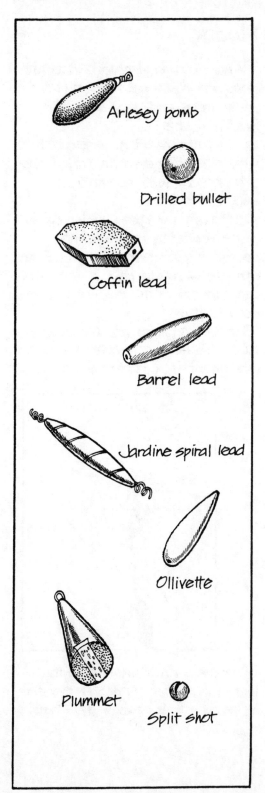

Arlesey bomb

Drilled bullet

Coffin lead

Barrel lead

Jardine spiral lead

Ollivette

Plummet

Split shot

•	No. 10
•	No. 8
•	No. 6
•	No. 4
•	No. 1
•	BB
•	AAA
•	SSG

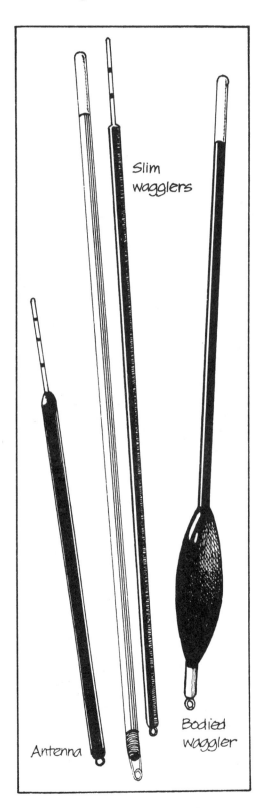

Slim
wagglers

Antenna

Bodied
waggler

Floats

Antenna and waggler floats are designed mainly for fishing on stillwaters and very slow—moving rivers.

The antenna float is used at very close range when conditions are perfect with no wind or surface drift.

Straight wagglers, which carry more shot than the antenna, permit longer-range fishing. Some straight wagglers have a very thin cane insert in the tip for greater sensitivity.

Bodied wagglers are for long-range fishing, or where surface movement is a problem.

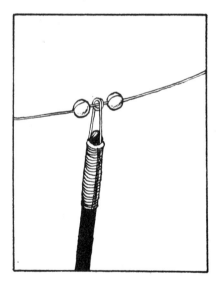

Wagglers are attached to the line by a split shot placed either side of the eye at the base of the float.

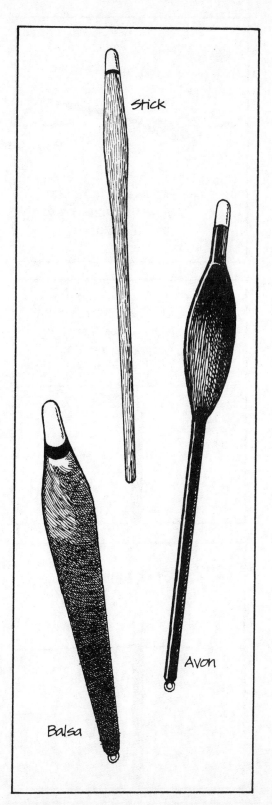

Stick, Avon and balsa floats are all intended for fishing on running water.

The stick float is used, with best results, not too far out from the rod tip and trotted down—stream. This slender float is ideal for roach, dace and chub.

The Avon, being more buoyant in the top area, can cope with a wider range of conditions than the stick. The ideal float for the beginner to learn the art of trotting the stream.

The balsa is the big brother of fast-water floats. In its larger sizes it is ideal for fishing big baits, like luncheon meat or worms, in deep, fast swims.

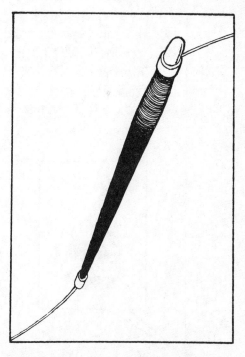

Sticks, Avons and balsas are all attached to the line top and bottom.

Finding the depth

If you intend to present your bait on, or very close to the bottom, the most accurate and positive way to achieve this is with the aid of a plummet.

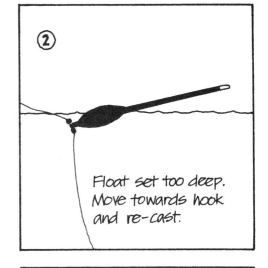

② Float set too deep. Move towards hook and re-cast.

① Estimate the depth and fix the float in position.
Hook a plummet to the end of the line by passing the hook through the eye at the top and inserting it into the cork at the base. Then cast to the area you intend to fish.

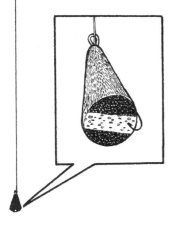

③ Float set too shallow. Move away from hook and re-cast.

④ Just right.

Sinking the line

Whenever a waggler is being used
the line must always be submerged
between the rod tip and the float.

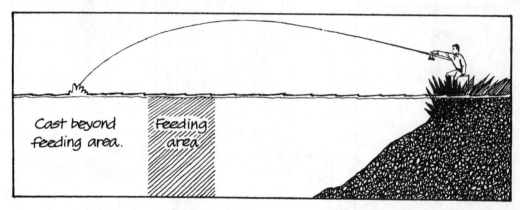

Cast beyond feeding area.

Feeding area

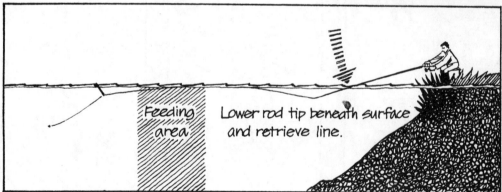

Feeding area

Lower rod tip beneath surface
and retrieve line.

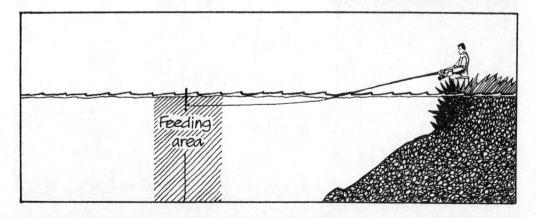

Feeding area

Shotting patterns

Stillwater

Each type of float is made in a variety of sizes; therefore it would be confusing to quote specific sizes in shot.

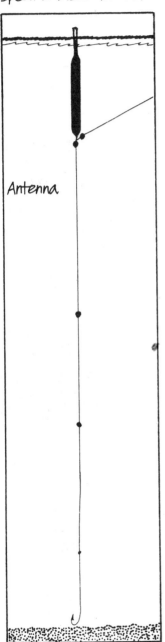

Antenna

Straight waggler

Bodied waggler

Running water

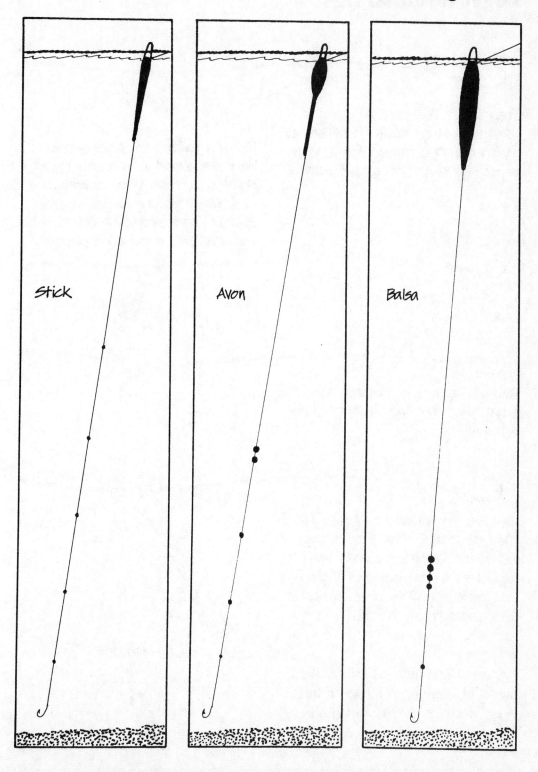

Stick

Avon

Balsa

Leger terminal rigs

Free line: This very basic rig is used with large baits. It offers no resistance to a taking fish and is especially suited to carp fishing.

Running leger with Arlesey bomb: With the added weight this rig is capable of fishing baits both large and small at long range. A split shot or leger stop is used to hold the lead in the required position.

Running leger with drilled bullet: Ideal for trundling a bait down-stream.

Running link leger with Arlesey bomb: This rig enables the fish to take more line before it comes up against the resistance of the bomb, and in the process gives an early bite register at the rod.

A very light link leger can be made by squeezing two or three swan shot on to the nylon link.

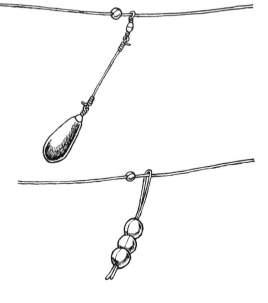

Leger terminal rigs

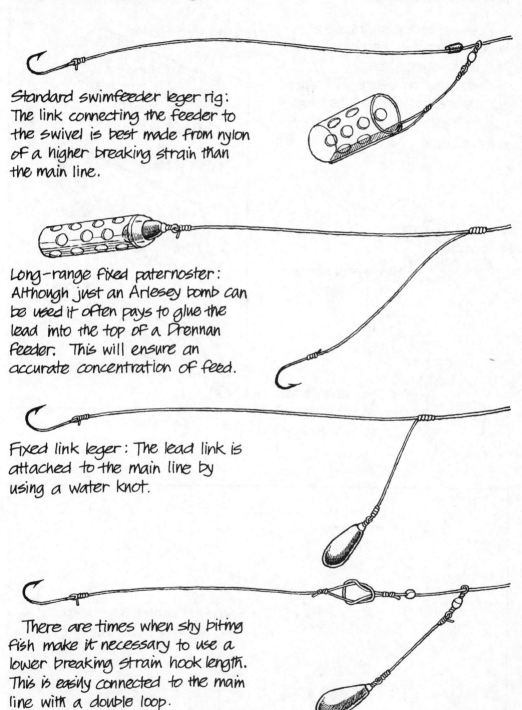

Standard swimfeeder leger rig:
The link connecting the feeder to
the swivel is best made from nylon
of a higher breaking strain than
the main line.

Long-range fixed paternoster:
Although just an Arlesey bomb can
be used it often pays to glue the
lead into the top of a Drennan
feeder. This will ensure an
accurate concentration of feed.

Fixed link leger: The lead link is
attached to the main line by
using a water knot.

There are times when shy biting
fish make it necessary to use a
lower breaking strain hook length.
This is easily connected to the main
line with a double loop.

Swimfeeders

A swimfeeder enables the angler to present the feed and the bait in the same area.

Concentration of the fish shoal will therefore increase the likeli-hood of the hook-bait being given some attention by the feeding fish.

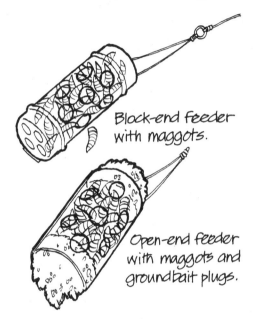

Block-end feeder with maggots.

Open-end feeder with maggots and groundbait plugs.

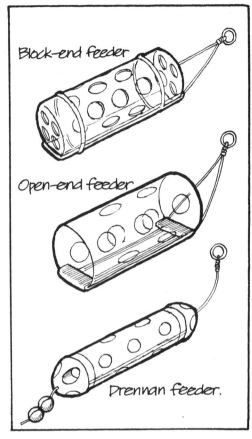

Block-end feeder

Open-end feeder

Drennan feeder.

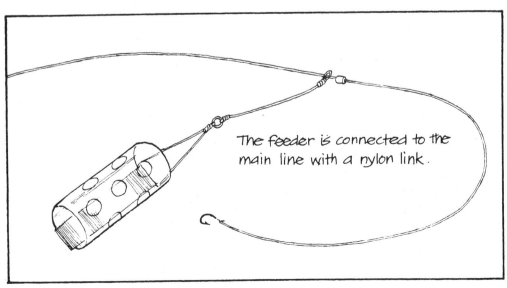

The feeder is connected to the main line with a nylon link.

Overhead cast

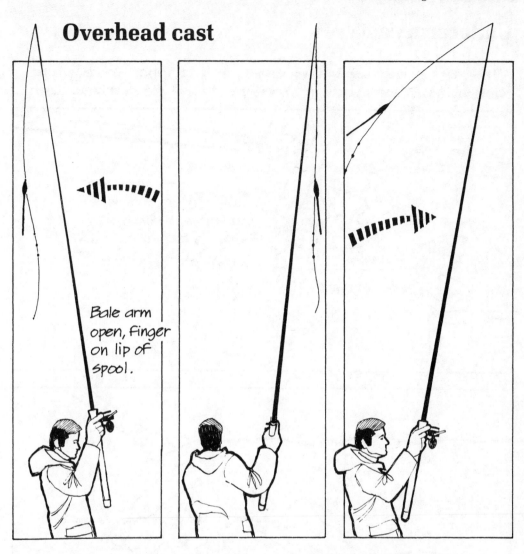

Bale arm open, finger on lip of spool.

As terminal tackle flies past rod tip, lift finger from spool to release line.

Follow through to this position; re-engage bale arm by turning reel handle.

Underarm cast

This cast is most useful when fishing in a confined space, where overhanging foliage makes it impossible to use the overhead cast.

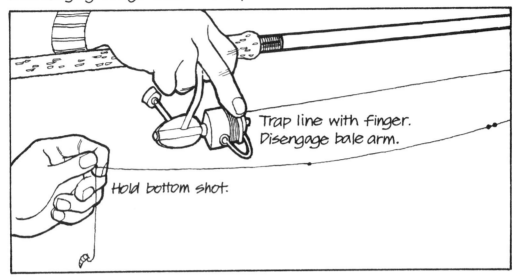

Trap line with finger.
Disengage bale arm.

Hold bottom shot.

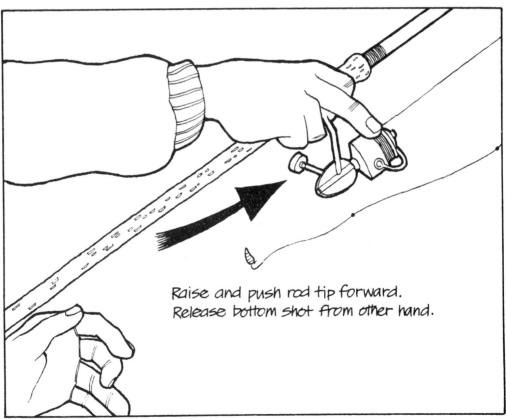

Raise and push rod tip forward.
Release bottom shot from other hand.

Underarm cast

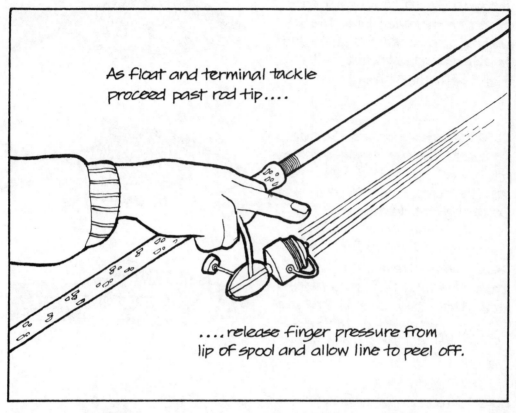

As float and terminal tackle proceed past rod tip....

....release finger pressure from lip of spool and allow line to peel off.

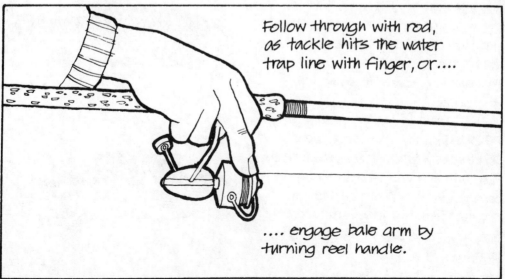

Follow through with rod, as tackle hits the water trap line with finger, or....

.... engage bale arm by turning reel handle.

Species

ROACH: A very common fish found in most lowland lakes and rivers. The eye is quite red, with tinges of red on the lower fins. The general body colour is silver, but on older, larger specimens it might be rather brassy.

RUDD: A deeper bodied fish than the roach. The eye is gold and the pelvic, anal and tail fins are bright red. The pelvic fins are positioned forward of the dorsal fin.

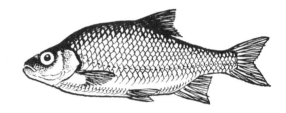

DACE: More streamlined than the roach, this little fish likes running water, but is also found in some lakes. The eye is yellowish, and the edge of the anal fin is concave.

CHUB: The anal fin is convex— a sure means of identification when compared with a dace. They like running water, especially where trees overhang the river. They are also found in some lakes.

PERCH: Found in lowland lakes, ponds and rivers. It is a handsome fish with a row of spines along the dorsal fin, and some on the gill covers. The body is generally green. The pelvic and anal fins are vivid red.

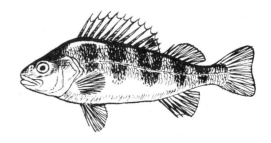

BRONZE BREAM : Very slow moving rivers, lakes and canals are the haunts of this fish, which is never happier than when rooting around in mud. Its protractile mouth enables it to suck in small organisms from the soft bottom.

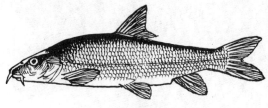

BARBEL : A powerful fish found in clear, fast-running water. Favoured haunts are weir-pools, depressions in the river-bed and beneath under-cut banks.

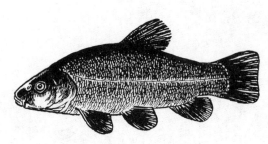

TENCH : Found in very slow rivers and lakes, where it feeds on the bottom. Quite often though it will show itself on the surface. Colour is predominantly olive, and the eye is small and red.

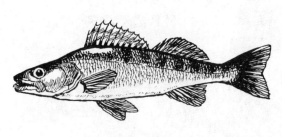

ZANDER : A fierce predator which prefers to hunt its prey in open water. The younger fish hunt in shoals, but as they grow larger a more solitary existence is adopted. Like the pike this fish is armed with a set of sharp fangs. It prefers still or very sluggish, murky water.

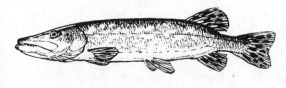

PIKE : Another fierce predator, but having a preference for weed beds where it lies in wait for its prey, which is just about any species of fish. It will not hesitate to attack a member of its own species.

CARP: A dweller of lakes, ponds and slow rivers. Three varieties of cultivated carp exist, namely the COMMON, MIRROR and LEATHER. If left to breed in a wild state, the offspring will revert to the original slim shape of the WILD CARP.

Species

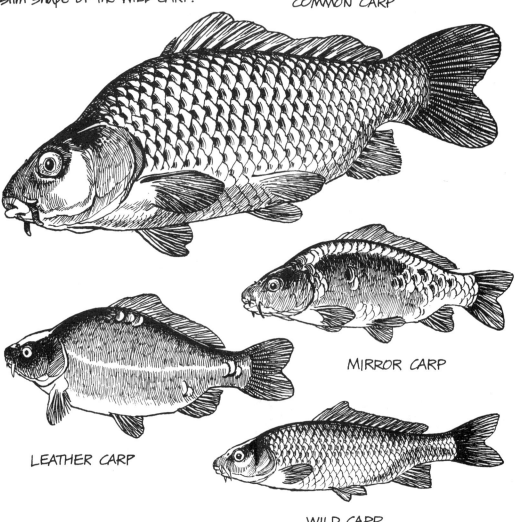

COMMON CARP

MIRROR CARP

LEATHER CARP

WILD CARP

The habits of these varieties of carp are identical, and the same fishing tactics can be employed for all of them. The wild carp does not grow to such a large size as the common, leather or mirror varieties, but what it lacks in size is more than compensated for in speed.

CRUCIAN CARP: This hardy species never grows to any great size, but will often thrive in waters where other species cannot. It lacks barbels, and feeds mainly on the bottom.

EEL: Found just about anywhere with enough water to cover its back. Shallow, weedy lakes and ponds seem to provide the really large specimens. Waters holding a large population of stunted fodder fish, such as roach, rudd or bleak are sure to support big eels.

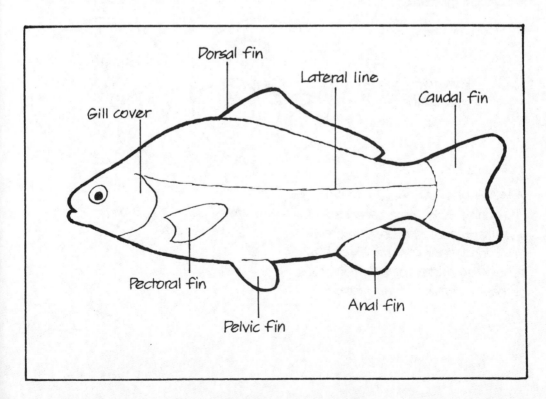

Dorsal fin

Lateral line

Caudal fin

Gill cover

Pectoral fin

Pelvic fin

Anal fin

Baits

MAGGOT: Without a doubt the most widely-used bait for coarse fish. More than one type of maggot can be bought commercially. The main one is the larvae of the blow fly, and is used mainly as a hook bait. Pinkies and squatts are smaller and are used as feeder maggots. Another type is the gozzer, which is an excellent bait for bream. To keep maggots at their best store them in a cool place.

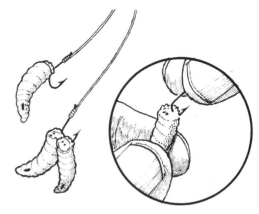

To hook a maggot, squeeze gently between finger and thumb. Nick the hook into the flap of frilly skin.

CASTER: The next stage of metamorphosis before the maggot becomes an adult fly. They are ideal as loose feed and are often mixed with groundbait. If used as a hook bait they are very likely to produce better quality fish.

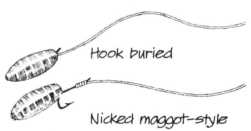

Hook buried

Nicked maggot-style

How to bury a hook in a caster.

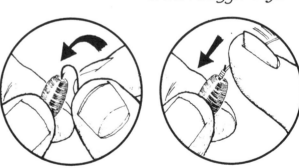

WASP GRUB: An excellent bait for chub, and many other species. To acquire them is no easy matter. Your local pest control expert may be able to supply you with a couple of nests complete with grubs.

LOBWORM: Definitely a big fish bait. Walk out on to a lawn on a warm night, with a torch, and if the ground is moist you will see them lying full length on the grass with just the tips of their tails in their holes. If you are stealthy, you can fill a bait container in a very short time. They are best kept in damp moss or newspaper.

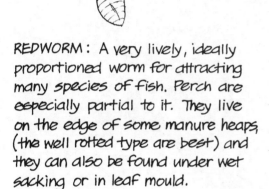

REDWORM: A very lively, ideally proportioned worm for attracting many species of fish. Perch are especially partial to it. They live on the edge of some manure heaps, (the well rotted type are best) and they can also be found under wet sacking or in leaf mould.

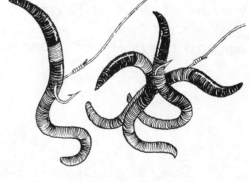

BRANDLING: Another very lively worm found in manure heaps. Fish take them readily enough, but they are rather unpleasant to use as they exude a pungent yellow liquid, when the hook is inserted. Unless you have no other choice they are best left in the manure heap. Mount them on the hook as you would a redworm.

BREAD FLAKE: Fresh bread is best suited for this. Simply pinch out a piece of bread from the middle portion of the loaf. Squeeze part of it on to the rear end of the hook shank, but leave the bread which covers the bend of the hook in its natural state.

BREAD CRUST: A very versatile bait. It can be used floating on the surface, resting on a sub-merged weedbed, or floating just off the bottom. A bait favoured by many big fish hunters.

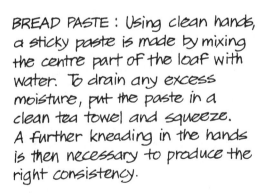

BREAD PASTE: Using clean hands, a sticky paste is made by mixing the centre part of the loaf with water. To drain any excess moisture, put the paste in a clean tea towel and squeeze. A further kneading in the hands is then necessary to produce the right consistency.

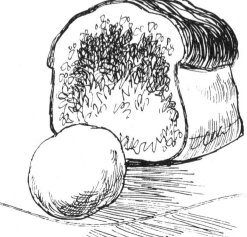

LUNCHEON MEAT: An excellent bait for barbel and chub.

CHEESE: This is one of the old favourites; some anglers use nothing else. The wide variety gives plenty of scope for experiment. As cheese tends to harden after being submerged in water it is best to test the consistency, to ensure that the hook will penetrate through the bait when the strike is made.

POTATO: Used almost exclusively for carp, although if mashed and converted to paste form will interest many other species. New potatoes are the best type, and need to be boiled, but not to the extent where they start to crumble; remember, they have to stay on the hook during the stress of casting.

A baiting needle is used to pull the line through the potato. The hook is then tied to the line and pulled back until it is buried in the bait.

SWEETCORN: An excellent bait for carp and tench. Constantly buying the pre-cooked tinned variety can be expensive if it is used for loose feed as well as hook bait. However, by purchasing loose maize from your local corn merchant you can use this as loose feed, and by using the larger, tinned kernels on the hook the cost over the season will be considerably reduced.

HEMPSEED: On a water which is fished regularly with hemp, this is a deadly bait from the word go. On waters where its use is infrequent or unknown, it may take a while for the fish to become accustomed to it, but thereafter will have a devastating effect. Before use, it has to be soaked for twenty-four hours, or simmered for about forty-five minutes, until it splits.

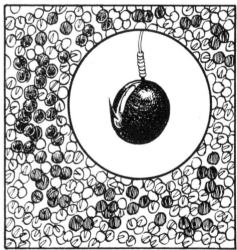

ELDERBERRY: Another very seasonal bait that will tempt roach, dace and occasionally bigger fish like chub and barbel. Loose feed three or four berries with every cast. Split shot should not be used in conjunction with hempseed or elder-berry. Instead use a twist of lead wire.

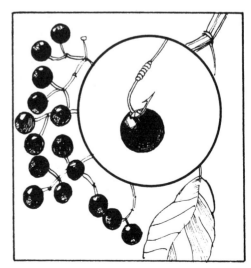

Groundbait

This is a mixture that is introduced into the swim you intend to fish, or are fishing. It can be introduced at regular intervals prior to the actual fishing day, (known as 'pre-baiting'). Tench respond to this treatment particularly well. Brown breadcrumb with water is a good base for groundbait.

When mixed with water it should have a consistency which allows it to be fashioned into golfball-sized balls, without crumbling. Samples of hookbait can be integrated with the base, eg., maggots or casters.

These balls are introduced by hand, or with the aid of a cata-pult, to the swim, where they dis-integrate. The introduction of more groundbait during the fishing session is sometimes necessary. Heavy groundbaiting can often do more harm than good. Little and often is a more sensible and pro-ductive policy.

Loose feed

Introduced into the swim during the process of fishing. The particles are usually, but not always, the same as the hook-bait.

Fish such as roach, rudd, dace and chub, will often rise towards the surface to intercept sinking feed particles, and in cases like this, fishing a slow-sinking bait works best (fishing on the drop).

Bottom-feeding fish such as tench, bream and carp, will be more likely to approach the loose feed as it lies on the bottom.

Bite indicators for legering

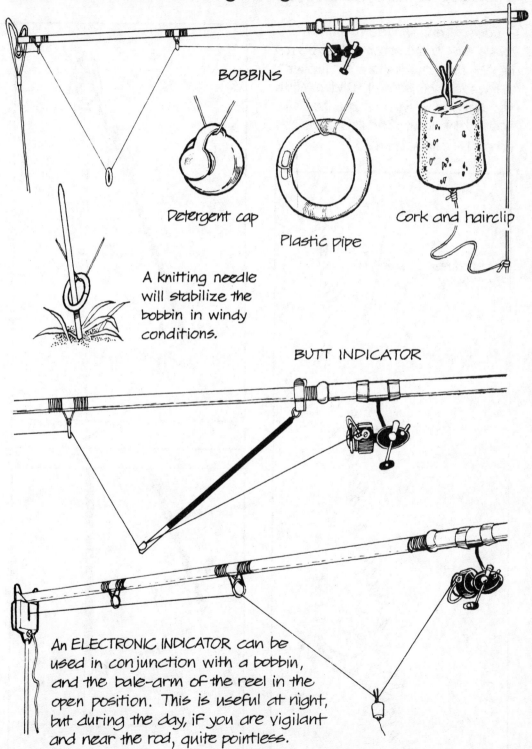

BOBBINS

Detergent cap

Plastic pipe

Cork and hairclip

A knitting needle will stabilize the bobbin in windy conditions.

BUTT INDICATOR

An ELECTRONIC INDICATOR can be used in conjunction with a bobbin, and the bale-arm of the reel in the open position. This is useful at night, but during the day, if you are vigilant and near the rod, quite pointless.

Fishing with a swingtip

Cast out and let the terminal tackle sink to the bottom. Place the rod on the rests and tighten the line with a few turns of the reel handle. When the swingtip is hanging off the vertical by about 25° it is in the correct fishing position.

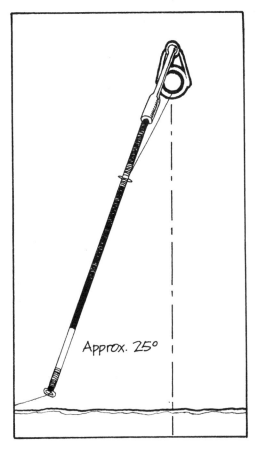

Approx. 25°

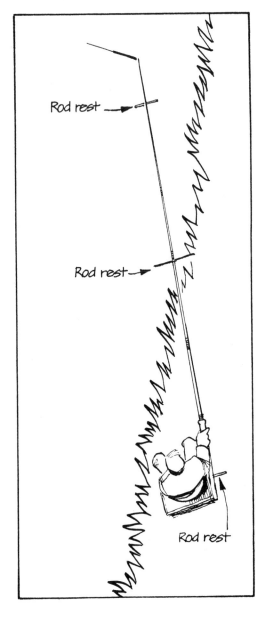

Rod rest

Rod rest

Rod rest

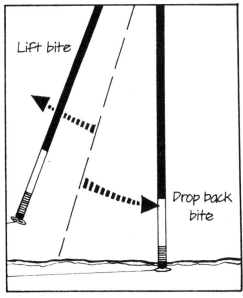

Lift bite

Drop back bite

Fishing with a quivertip

The quivertip has an advantage over the swingtip in as much as it can be used on running water as well as stillwater. For normal conditions, position the rod rests and rod as you would for a swingtip. After casting, tighten up to the lead so that the tip adopts a slight curve. This will enable the tip to straighten up when a drop-back bite occurs.

If you are fishing the far bank on a river and the current is strong in mid-stream, you can overcome the problem of water pressure affecting the sensitivity of the tip by propping up the rod. This will lift a lot of line clear of the water.

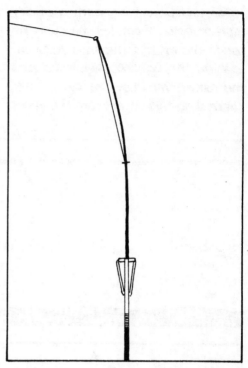

Attitude of quivertip after the line has been tightened – ready for a bite.

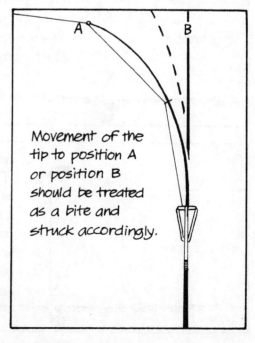

Movement of the tip to position A or position B should be treated as a bite and struck accordingly.

Trotting the stream

Suspend a bait beneath a stick, Avon or balsa float, let the current carry the end tackle in a natural fashion through the swim, and at the same time allow the pull of the current to take line from the spool of the reel. In the past, the centre-pin reel was used for this style of fishing, but nowadays the closed-face and fixed-spool reels are used more often than their predecessor.

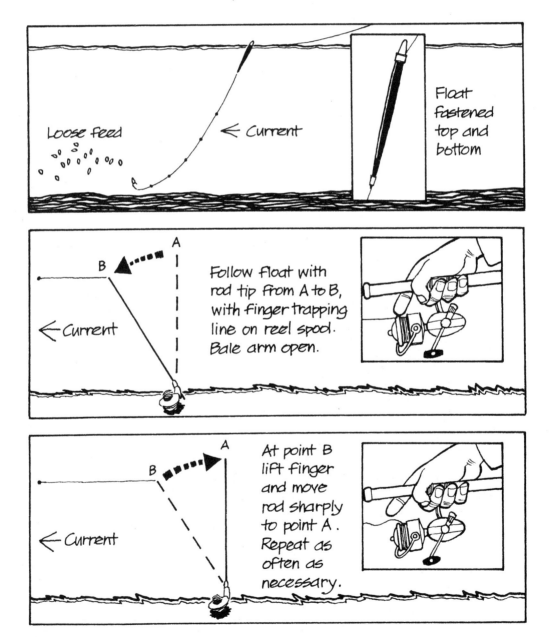

Loose feed

← Current

Float fastened top and bottom

B ◀······ A

← Current

Follow float with rod tip from A to B, with finger trapping line on reel spool. Bale arm open.

B ◀······ A

← Current

At point B lift finger and move rod sharply to point A. Repeat as often as necessary.

Mending the line

Trotting the stream directly down-stream from the rod tip is fairly straightforward, but the problem of a bow in the line presents itself if the bait is being fished well out from the rod tip. If the bow is ignored the pressure of the current will build up within the bow and pull the float and bait across the stream in a most unnatural manner. Mending the line will cure this in its early stages.

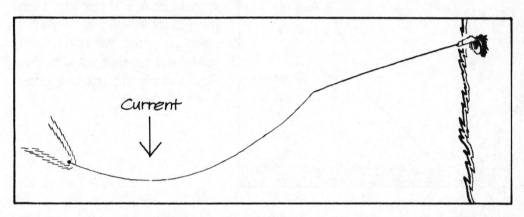

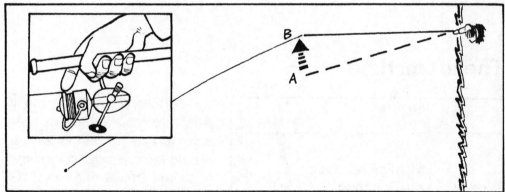

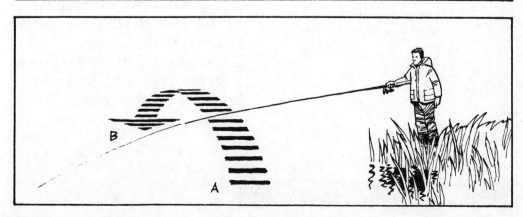

Laying on

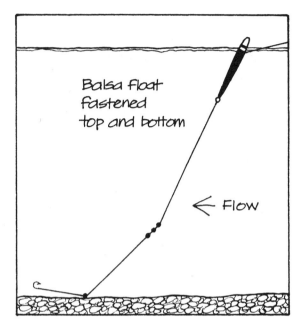

Balsa float
fastened
top and bottom

← Flow

This method is employed on running-waters. It comes into its own during winter, when the river is usually running higher, with a bit of colour. It is best to fish directly downstream from the rod tip. Set the float over-depth. After casting, place the rod in a rest, and tighten-up until the float adopts the attitude shown in the diagram.

The lift method

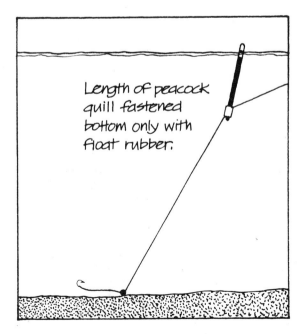

Length of peacock
quill fastened
bottom only with
float rubber.

A stillwater method, ideally suited to tench. The float is set over-depth and a large single shot is pinched on the line just above the hook. As with the above method, the rod must be placed in a rest until a bite occurs.

A typical lift-bite is signalled by the float lying flat on the surface, but occasionally it just slides out of sight.

Slider float

Used when the depth being fished is greater than the length of the rod, or when bankside foliage restricts overarm casting. For fishing still-waters a large-bodied waggler is employed as a slider, while on running water a special balsa float with two rings is used.

In order to stop the float at the required distance above the bait, a sliding stop knot is tied onto the main line.

SLIDING STOP KNOT

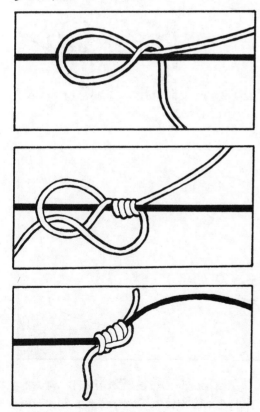

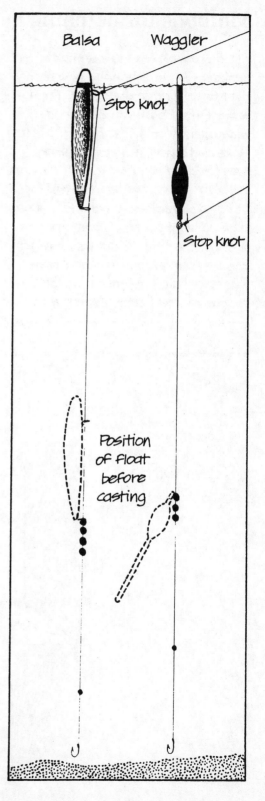

Balsa   Waggler

Stop knot

Stop knot

Position of float before casting

Methods for catching

Roach

It is probably true to say that more anglers fish intentionally for roach than for any other species of fresh-water fish. Roach will accept a wide variety of baits. Bread (paste, flake and crust), maggot, caster, hemp, redworm, cheese and lobworm tail have all accounted for this fish.

Choice of hook-size will of course depend on the size of bait being used at the time. Stillwater roach can be found close to weed beds, where a bait presented on the bottom will be best to start with.

Maggot, caster, hemp, bread paste: Hook, size 16 or 18.

Bunch of maggots, redworm : size 14.

Lobworm tail, bread flake or crust: size 12 or 10.

Loose feed
or
cloud bait

Continual loose-feeding, however, may have the effect of drawing the fish up, whereupon 'Fishing on the drop' tactics can be employed.

Roach

Running-water roach should be looked for in eddies and slacker areas of water out of the main current.

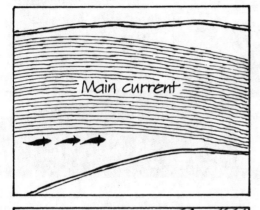

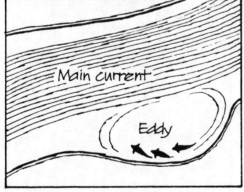

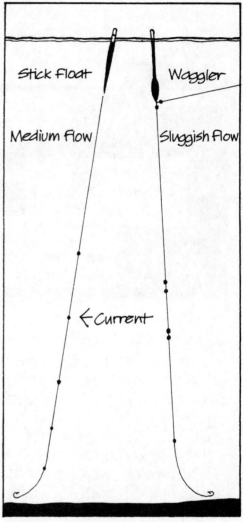

Running-water float tackle

Light leger tackle and a quiver-tip will produce roach, especially if the water is clearing after a flood.

Canal roach

TOW PATH

NEARSIDE SHELF

Start by fishing cloud groundbait and bread-punch hookbait....

... later, switch to hempseed further down the shelf.

BOAT CHANNEL
This area is usually unfishable unless boat traffic is very light, or during winter.

This bait will receive instant attention from the smaller roach which are often located on the top of the nearside shelf. A breadpunch tool will be required to cut the sliced bread into neat, little hook-sized pieces.

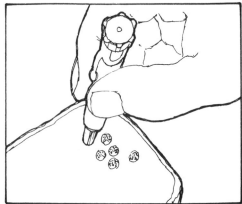

BREADPUNCH
with spare tips

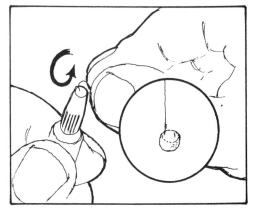

Loosefeed maggots via catapult from time-to-time as fish may be spooked from nearside shelf in clear water.

FAR SHELF

Always a good roach area, especially with overhanging foliage (eg., elderberry). Use a long pole or rod and waggler rig.

Legering on canals

Should windy weather make float presentation impossible, leger tactics will often prove very effective. A 6 or 7 ft (1·85 or 2·15 m) wand, used quivertip style, is easy to tuck behind the shelter of a fishing umbrella. A shot link leger will provide the end rig as long casts will not be necessary.

Rudd

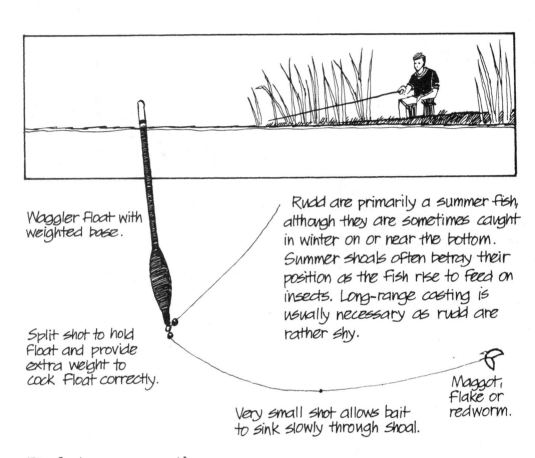

Waggler float with weighted base.

Rudd are primarily a summer fish, although they are sometimes caught in winter on or near the bottom. Summer shoals often betray their position as the fish rise to feed on insects. Long-range casting is usually necessary as rudd are rather shy.

Split shot to hold float and provide extra weight to cock float correctly.

Very small shot allows bait to sink slowly through shoal.

Maggot, Flake or redworm.

Rig for long-range casting

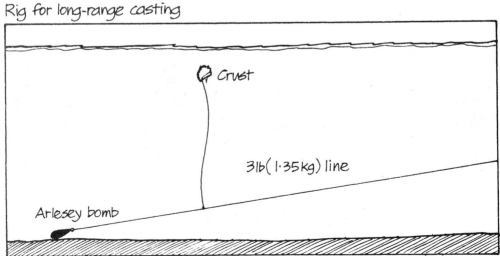

Crust

3lb (1·35kg) line

Arlesey bomb

The rudd, with its protruding bottom jaw, is well equipped for sucking insects from the surface film. Large shoals can often be seen feeding in this manner, so it is therefore logical, at such times, to present the bait in or just beneath the surface.

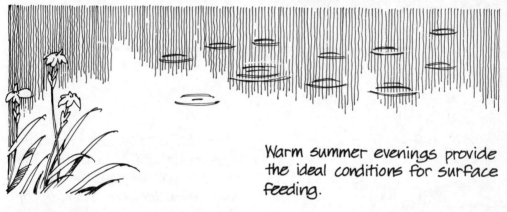

Warm summer evenings provide the ideal conditions for surface feeding.

SURFACE RIG FOR RUDD

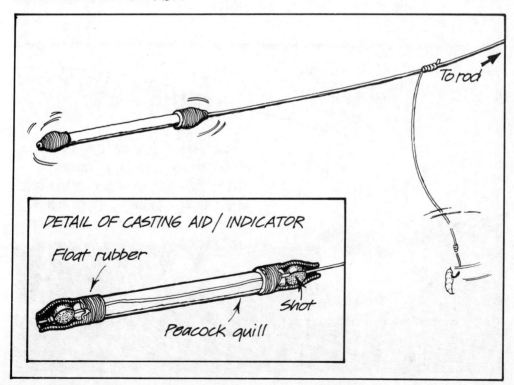

To rod

DETAIL OF CASTING AID / INDICATOR

Float rubber

Shot

Peacock quill

Dace

Dace form large shoals and can be found widely distributed over most rivers, sometimes accompanied by small chub. Their presence is often displayed by dimples on the surface as they rise to take insects.

A bait suspended beneath a stick float and preceded by loose-feed will usually attract these fast biters.

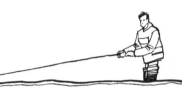

They can also be taken on light leger tackle and a quivertip. This tackle is best employed in slack areas of water near the bank, or where a shallow runs into deeper water.

Two swan shot
link leger

Dace found in these quieter areas of water tend to be a better stamp of fish, and will often bite more boldly, taking larger baits such as bread flake or redworm.

Dace

Dace respond very well to a dry fly, but the angler will need lightening-fast reflexes to hook this little silver darter.

For maximum sport, use a 7ft (2·15m) carbon fly rod teamed with a Nº4 double-tapered floating line and a 7–9ft (2·15–2·75m) leader with a fine point. Flies need to be small, tied to size 16–18 hooks.

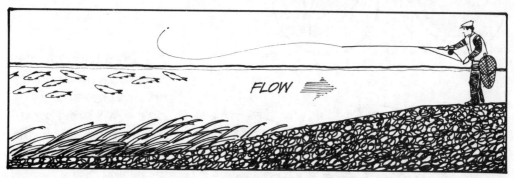

FLOW

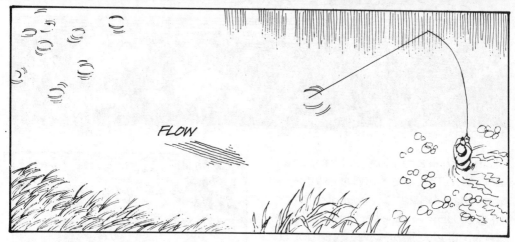

FLOW

Cast the fly to the tail-end of the rising shoal. Hooked fish can then be drawn downstream and played out without disturbing the remainder of the shoal.

A few suggested patterns

Tup's Indispensable

Greenwell's Glory

Black Gnat

Grey Duster

Chub

Small chub are gregarious, and can form large shoals. Without knowing what to look for it is easy to confuse a small chub with a large dace. The key to positive identification lies in the anal fin.

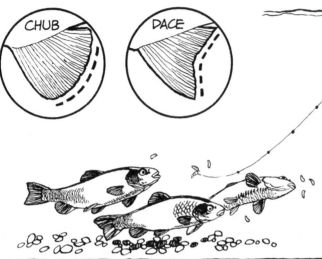

Trotting the stream with a stick or Avon float is a good way of getting to grips with these smaller chub.

A legered bait fished in conjunction with a quiver tip, and presented fairly close in will bring good results, especially in the winter when the river is running high.

Large chub are more solitary, and very shy. They like to have a roof over their heads. Overhanging trees, rafts of driftwood, overhanging banks, are all likely chub spots. Just let a leger roll into these sorts of places. If there is no response after a while, then move on to another chubby-looking hole. Here are just a few chub baits: maggots, casters, bread, cheese, luncheon meat, wasp grubs, crayfish, slugs and worms.

Chub

A large, bushy artificial fly cast under, or close to overhanging bushes, will often account for large chub.

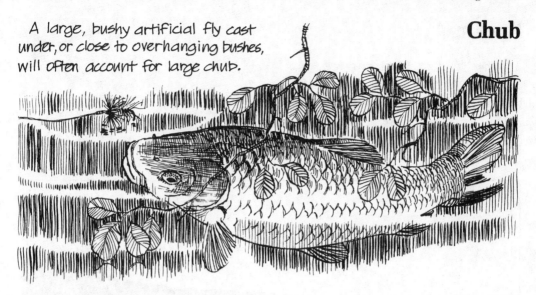

Chub living in very small streams are often visible, and wary, therefore the angler should proceed with extreme caution. It is best to fish freelined baits, presenting the offering just behind the fish. It does not matter if the bait makes a splash as it hits the water, for this usually results in the fish making a quick turn, and grabbing the bait confidently.

Some huge chub exist in certain stillwaters. Illustrated below is the unconventional tackle used for the capture of a 7lb (3.00 kg) specimen from an Oxfordshire gravel pit.

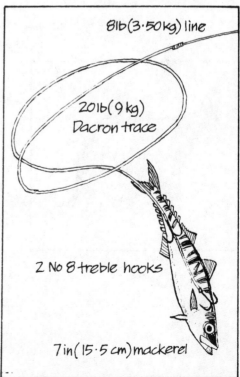

8lb (3.50 kg) line

20lb (9 kg) Dacron trace

2 No 8 treble hooks

7 in (15.5 cm) mackerel

Bream

Bream tend to shoal and feed in depressions on the river or lake bed. Where shallower water starts to drop away into deeper water is always a good place to present your bait.

Introduce some balls of groundbait into the swim prior to fishing.

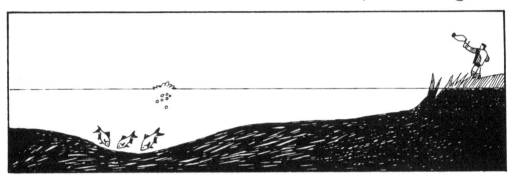

2-3lb hook link (1·35 kg)

Hook size 18-12

Arlesey bomb

Terminal leger tackle

3-4lb main line (1·80 kg)

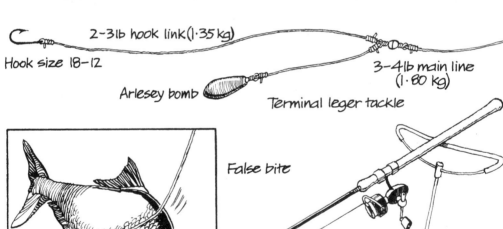

False bite

False bites are all too common when the bait is lying in a dense shoal of bream, and some of them look very convincing on the bite indicator. The solution is to have the bobbin suspended well down from the rod and to resist the temptation to strike until it has risen all the way.
Baits: Maggots, Bread flake, Redworms.

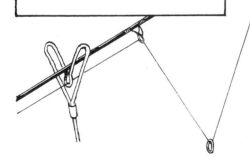

Bream

Locating a shoal of feeding bream can be a problem, as they tend to roam, and will not necessarily be in the same swim two days running. Making a reconnaissance of the river or lake may well save hours of fruitless fishing.

When bream can be seen priming on the surface, it is an indication that a shoal will be feeding in that area.

Another giveaway is an area of discoloured water, with perhaps bubbles on the surface.

Introduce loose feed to the near side of the shoal, and fish in that area. Any hooked fish does not then have to be played right through the shoal.

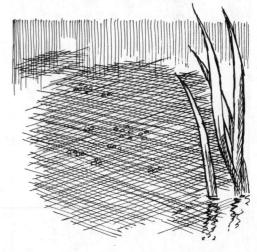

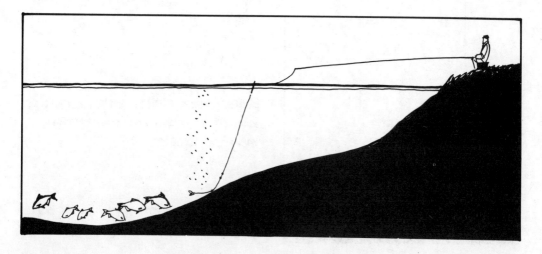

Tench

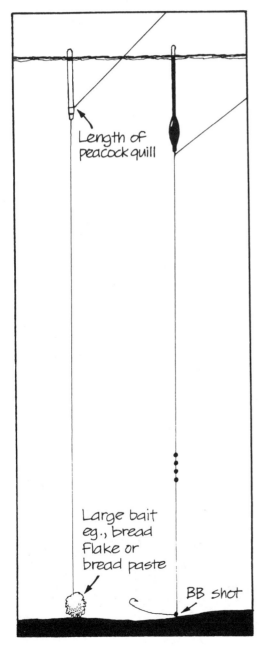

Leger terminal tackle can be the same as that used for bream.

Length of peacock quill

Large bait eg., bread Flake or bread paste

BB shot

This, more than any other, is a fish of summer. A dawn session, prior to a hot day, will usually bring the best results. Tench will, however, continue to feed right through the day if it is overcast and mild.

It is good policy to groundbait your swim daily, prior to fishing.

If weedgrowth is very prolific, a rake pulled through the swim will clear most of it and will also disturb the bottom, which in turn will attract fish into the area.

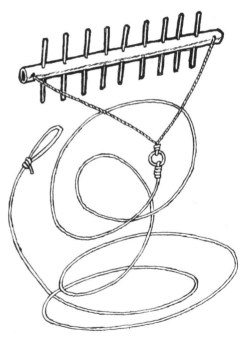

Baits: Bread flake, paste and crust, lobworm, redworm, sweetcorn, maggot, caster.

The tench float rig will also serve very well for catching bream.

Tench

The tench also creates bubbles during the process of feeding, although the absence of bubbles does not indicate that fishing is a waste of time. I have caught good bags of tench with not a bubble in sight.

Float fishing is the most popular and enjoyable method for taking this delightful fish.

Typical tench bite

Groundbait introduced to this area for two days prior to fishing.

Barbel

Like the carp, this is another fish that requires a special type of rod. The combination of a powerful fish and its environment (fast-flowing water) will necessitate using a rod with a through action.

The rod should be about 11ft (3·35m) in length.

An Avon float will cope with the smaller baits and medium-depth swims, but a balsa will be required for large baits and deep swims with a heavy flow.

Baits: Maggot, hempseed, worms, sausage, luncheon meat, cheese.

A rolling leger is the ideal method with which to search deep holes and weirpods, favourite barbel haunts. Use just enough lead to keep the tackle down, but not enough to hold bottom.

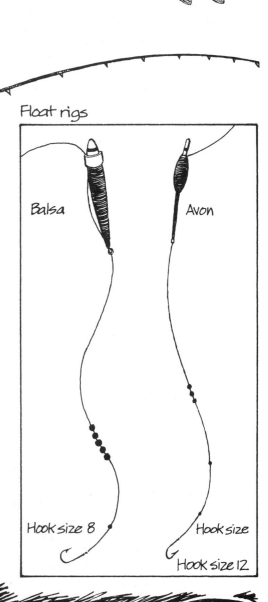

Float rigs

Balsa

Avon

Hook size 8

Hook size

Hook size 12

Barbel

Barbel also respond particularly well to swimfeeder tactics.

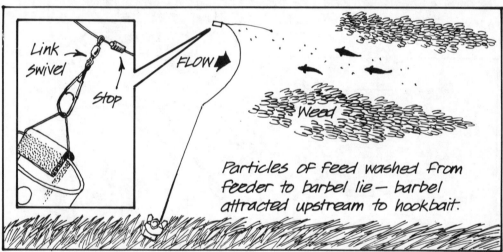

Link swivel

Stop

FLOW

Weed

Particles of feed washed from feeder to barbel lie – barbel attracted upstream to hookbait.

If the river is running high, position the rod tip well up for better control.

Pike

For the occasional pike session a carp rod will suffice, for casting small dead-baits, and spinning; but for regular use something a bit heavier will be needed. A stepped-up carp rod with a test curve of 2½ lb (1·10 kg) will be far more suitable.

Probably the most sporting and most enjoyable way of taking pike is by fishing a plug, or a lure.

Here is a small selection of the many patterns obtainable today.

Light-line plug fishing is usually practised with a short bait-casting rod, coupled with a multiplier or an Abumatic reel.

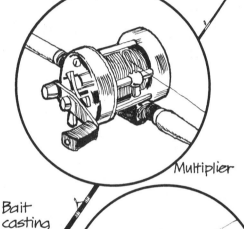

Multiplier

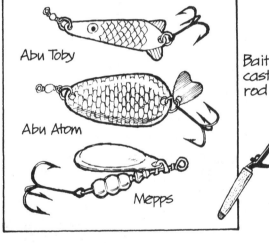

Lures

Abu Toby

Abu Atom

Mepps

Bait casting rod

Abumatic

When using lures that spin, it is advisable to attach an anti-kink device, or lead, to the line, in order to prevent line twist.

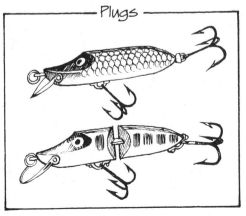

Plugs

Wye lead

Fold-over lead

'Anti-kink' ball bearing swivel

Spoons

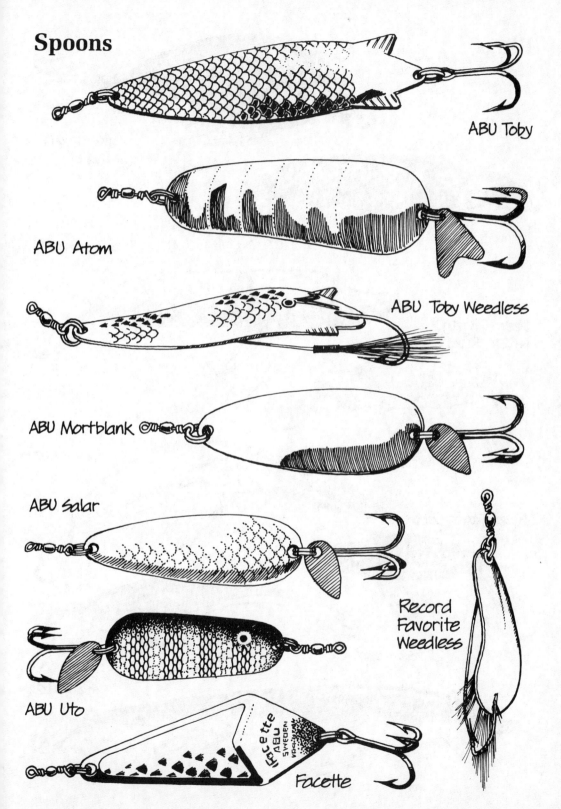

ABU Toby

ABU Atom

ABU Toby Weedless

ABU Mortblank

ABU Salar

Record
Favorite
Weedless

ABU Uto

Facette

Plugs

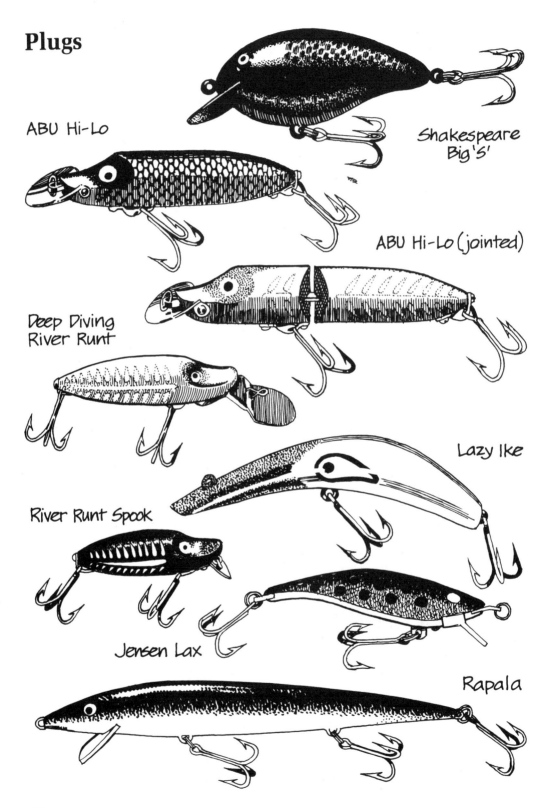

ABU Hi-Lo

Shakespeare Big 'S'

ABU Hi-Lo (jointed)

Deep Diving River Runt

Lazy Ike

River Runt Spook

Jensen Lax

Rapala

Pike

Some plugs sink slowly under their own weight; others float on the surface when stationary, but dive and wobble when retrieved. Their action is very typical of a small wounded fish, and irresistible to a hungry pike.

Swivel

18in (45cm) cable-laid wire approx. 20lb (9 kg) test.

Fishing with a static deadbait is likely to produce the really large specimens. To start with, you will need a collection of wire traces, and it is best if you make your own.

Two size 8 trebles

←3in (7·5cm)→

Bait: Roach, rudd, bleak, trout, mackerel, herring, sprat.

How to mount a legered deadbait.

A legered deadbait can also be fished in conjunction with a float.

Stop knot

Bead

Swan shot

Balsa pike float

67

Fishing a wobbled deadbait

During the autumn, shallow areas of a lake still support dense areas of bottom weed. These areas can be fished by working a deadbait just beneath the surface. Baits for this type of fishing should not be too large — 5in (12·5cm) is about right. To make the bait buoyant, insert a piece of polystyrene into the fish before it is mounted on the trace.

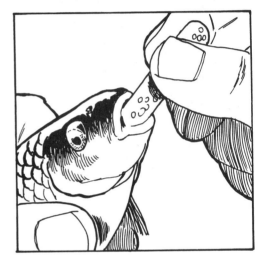

Wobble can be created by bending the body of the bait just before inserting the end treble. However, this can be overdone, producing an unnatural, gyrating motion when the bait is retrieved. The diagram(right) shows the subtle curve that is needed in order to produce the slow, natural, tumbling motion, typical of a wounded fish.

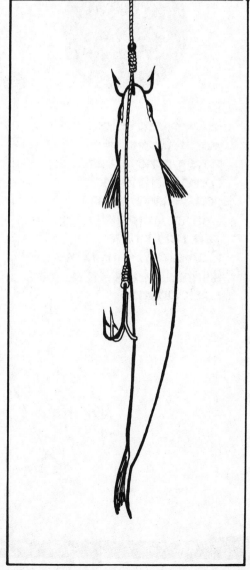

Float paternoster set-up

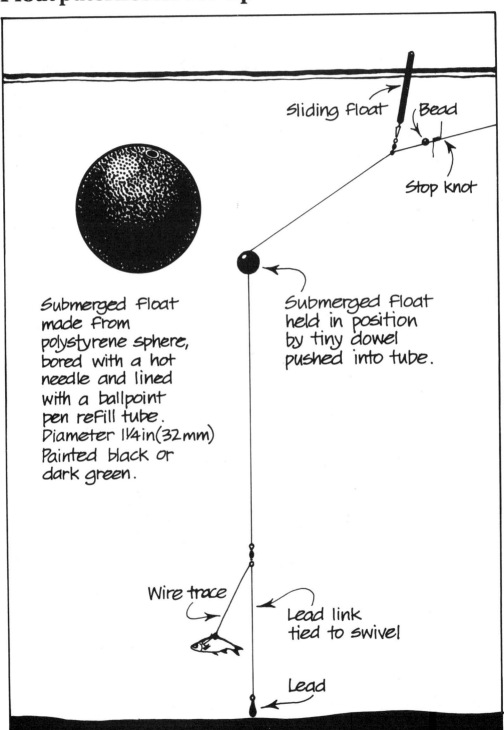

Sliding float

Bead

Stop knot

Submerged float made from polystyrene sphere, bored with a hot needle and lined with a ballpoint pen refill tube. Diameter 1¼in(32mm) Painted black or dark green.

Submerged float held in position by tiny dowel pushed into tube.

Wire trace

Lead link tied to swivel

Lead

Perch

Small to medium-sized perch are very rapacious, and can be caught on the most basic of tackle. They congregate close to weed beds, piles, sunken tree limbs and roots, etc.

A redworm is probably the best bait for these smaller predators.

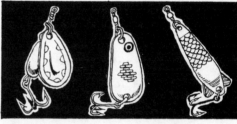

Perch will readily take a small spinner or spoon. A leger rod can be used for this form of fishing.

A selection of perch lures.

Large perch lead a more solitary existence, preferring to lurk in the deeper areas of lakes. Long-distance casting is often required to reach the perch holes, therefore the use of a leger rig will be necessary.

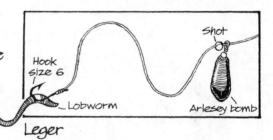

Leger

Running paternoster

Perch

The best time to fish for large stillwater perch is during the winter months. At this time of the year natural food is scarce and hook-baits are taken readily. Locating these deep water predators is not so easy, as they tend to concentrate in small areas in the deepest parts of the lake. Here is a simple and effective procedure for finding the likely 'hot-spots' where the really big perch lie during winter.

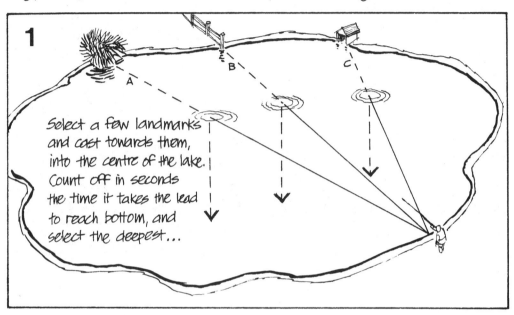

1

Select a few landmarks and cast towards them, into the centre of the lake. Count off in seconds the time it takes the lead to reach bottom, and select the deepest...

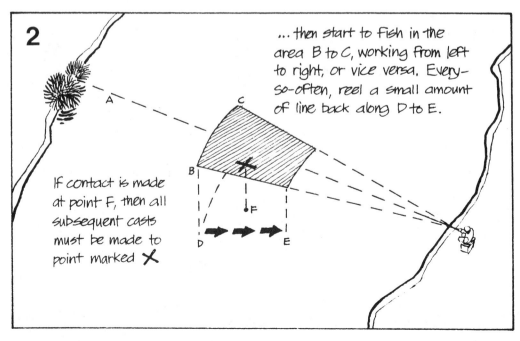

2

... then start to fish in the area B to C, working from left to right, or vice versa. Every-so-often, reel a small amount of line back along D to E.

If contact is made at point F, then all subsequent casts must be made to point marked ✗

Perch

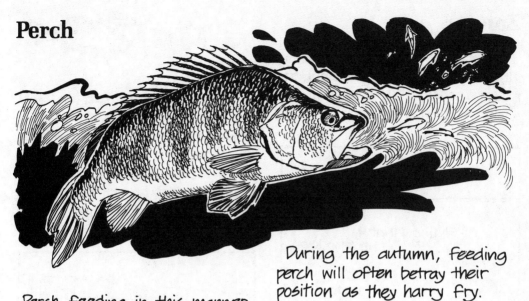

During the autumn, feeding perch will often betray their position as they harry fry.

Perch, feeding in this manner, can be caught with a small spinner or spoon, but fly tackle can also be employed to good effect. A fry-imitating lure, such as a Sinfoil's Fry, fished in conjunction with a floating or very slow sink line should provide interesting sport.

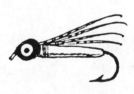

SINFOIL'S FRY

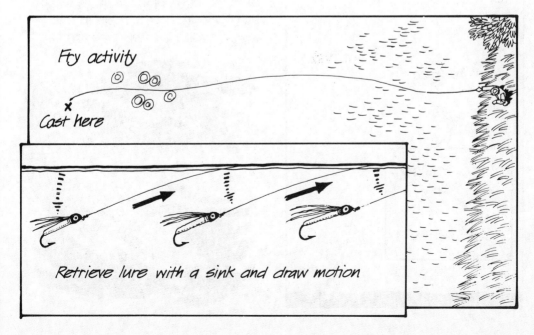

Fry activity

Cast here

Retrieve lure with a sink and draw motion

Zander

The tackle employed for catching pike can also be used for zander, except perhaps the hooks, which should be a size smaller.

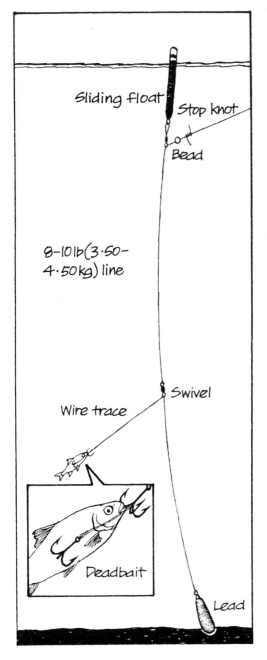

Sliding float

Stop knot

Bead

8–10 lb (3·50–4·50 kg) line

Swivel

Wire trace

Deadbait

Lead

When legering for zander (and pike), it is a good policy to leave the bale arm of the reel in the open position; this enables the fish to run freely with the bait. Whilst waiting for a bite the line can be kept taught by wedging it beneath a line clip.. A run will pull the line free.

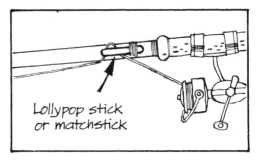

Lollypop stick or matchstick

Zander will readily attack a spinner or a plug. It is generally more productive to fish in open water, well clear of weedbeds.

Eel

Eels, especially small ones, can be a nuisance when they gorge a bait intended for other fish. Medium to large specimens, however, when specifically pursued, can provide a unique and exciting form of fishing.

A carp rod will be necessary for hauling this powerful fish away from underwater snags.

Legering at night, or during the day if the weather is humid and overcast, will produce the best results.

Terminal tackle

Swivel

12 in (30 cm) Wire trace

10 lb (4·50 kg) main line

Small Artesey bomb for casting a worm

Link swivel

Wire trace

Split shot prevents bait from sliding up the trace.

Hook size 2

Dead roach, rudd, bleak or dace, 4 in (10 cm) in length.

Lobworms

There is usually no need for any additional weight when using a dead fish bait. It will be necessary, however, to puncture the bladder of the dead fish, so that it sinks.

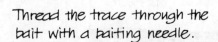

Thread the trace through the bait with a baiting needle.

75

Crucian carp

This sporting little fish which never grows to any great size 3lb (1·35kg) is about average), can be taken on similar tackle to that used for roach.

If surface drift becomes a problem, fasten the float bottom only, and/or use a slightly larger float and split shot.

Cloud groundbait as for roach.

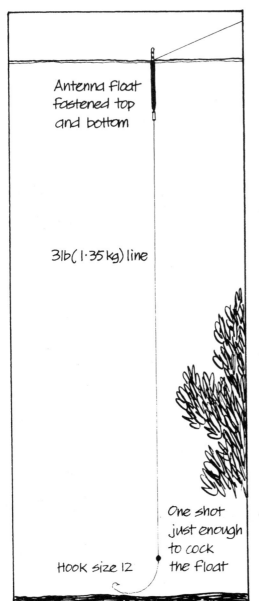

Antenna float fastened top and bottom

3lb (1·35 kg) line

One shot just enough to cock the float

Hook size 12

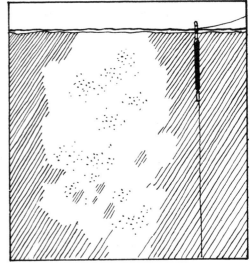

Baits

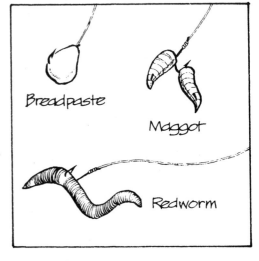

Breadpaste

Maggot

Redworm

Carp

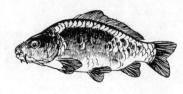

The carp is a very powerful fish, requiring an equally powerful rod to cope with his fury, when hooked.

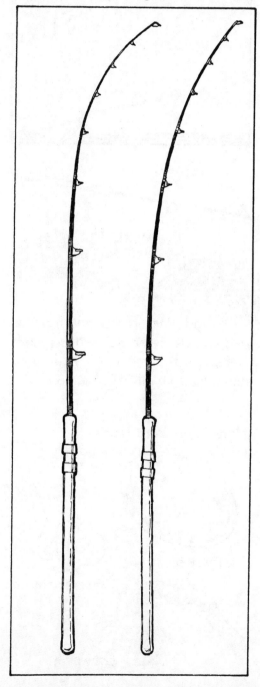

Floating bread crust

When carp are visible on the surface, this is the best method to use. A sandwich loaf makes the best floating crusts.

A gap in or alongside a weedbed is a good position for a crust.

When a carp takes the crust, don't panic and strike prematurely — wait until the line begins to run out across the surface of the water.

Carp

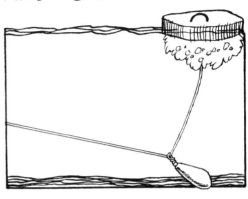

Anchored crust

Suspended crust

Mount the crust on the hook as before. Hold the crust under water and squeeze out the air.

Leger tackle should be kept as basic as possible.

At night, carp patrol the margins and can be tempted with a crust fished in this manner. The indicator is a length of silver foil.

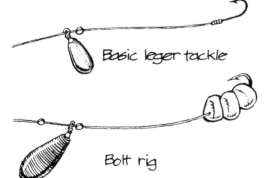

Basic leger tackle

Bolt rig

Finicky carp can be difficult to hook. When a bolt rig is used, the fish panics when it feels the hook, and makes a positive run.

More good carp baits

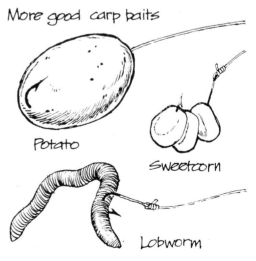

Potato

Sweetcorn

Lobworm

Fishing in weedy areas with a floating bait calls for absolute vigilance. A carp can suck in a bait, move away and eject it all within the space of a few seconds, very seldom returning for a second helping.

It can also be a mistake to tighten into a taking fish too early, but it is easily done, especially when a fish suddenly takes the bait after a long period of inactivity. The most accurate yardstick is to watch the line between the rod tip and the water level. Strike immediately when the line starts to move away.

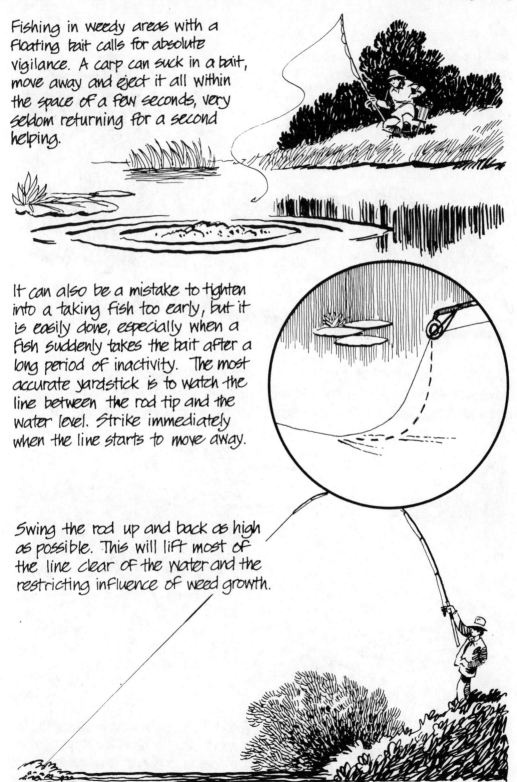

Swing the rod up and back as high as possible. This will lift most of the line clear of the water and the restricting influence of weed growth.

IF a hooked carp dives into dense weed and refuses to move, no amount of rod pressure will bring it out. If, however, the rod is lowered, thus creating slack line the fish will invariably come free. The rod should then be immediately raised to its former position.

A certain amount of bullying is advisable when playing a carp in and around weed. If possible the carp should be played into a clear area (if one exists) and brought to the net without undue delay.

When fishing in weedy areas it is a good idea to have an experienced companion present whose assistance will be invaluable.

How to play and land a fish

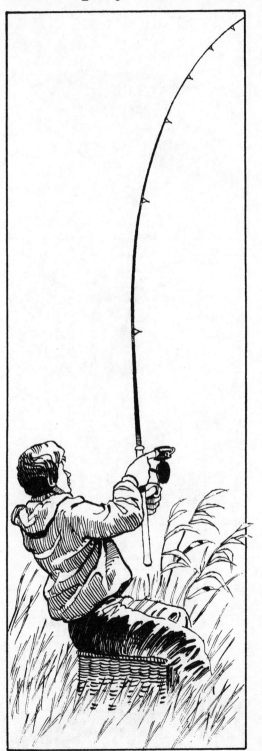

On hooking a fish, especially a large one, keep the rod tip well up and maintain a steady pressure. Never point the rod at the fish. The slipping clutch on the reel must be adjusted prior to fishing so that it yields line when the pressure on it is just below the breaking strain of the line.

If a hooked fish makes a dash for an area where underwater snags exist, it can be turned by applying side-strain.

Have the net close at hand. When the fish shows signs of tiring, slip the net into the water and keep it stationary. Never jab at the fish in an attempt to scoop it out. Bring the fish to the net, not the net to the fish.

Handling and hook removal

Always wet your hands before handling a fish. Grip the fish firmly but gently just behind the gill openings. If the hook is lightly embedded near the front of the mouth, it is possible to remove the hook with your finger-tips, otherwise use a disgorger.

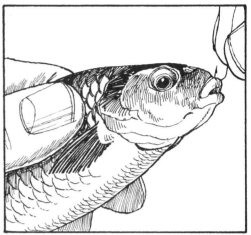

With larger fish, it is best to leave the fish lying in the damp net while you remove the hook. Artery forceps are best. When they are locked a really good grip is maintained on the hook, which can be gently eased out. A damp towel positioned between the hand and the fish is advisable, as large fish like carp are very strong and need some holding if they suddenly decide to leap about.

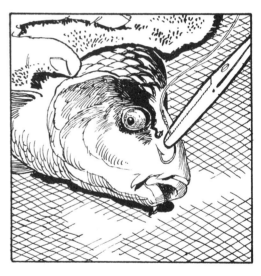

Deeply-hooked pike are best dealt with by inserting a pair of artery forceps through the gill opening. Extra care should be taken to avoid damaging the delicate gill rakers. Always wear a thick gardening glove on the left hand as protection against the pikes teeth.

Weighing a fish

The first requirement for this procedure is a knotless mesh bag or sling. This is saturated with water to prevent removal of protective slime from the fish. Place the sling on a soft base of grass or moss and gently slide the fish inside, first making sure that your hands are also wet. At a pinch, a landing net can be used (with the handle removed of course). Don't forget to allow for the weight of the landing net frame.

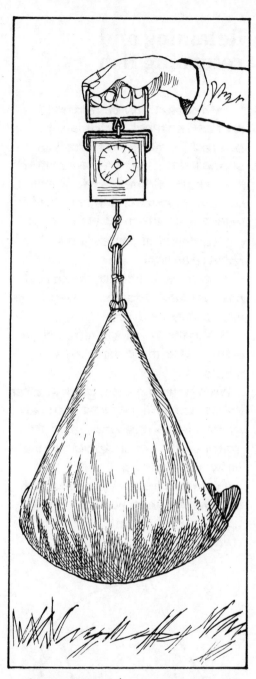

Fish weighed in this manner will lie quietly until the whole procedure is over.

Never weigh a live fish in this manner; it will damage the delicate gill filaments.

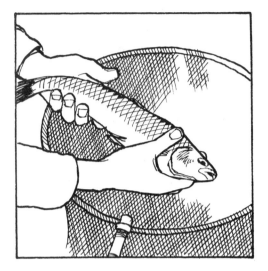

Retaining and returning fish

Fish should only be retained in a knotless keepnet, which is well covered by water, preferably in a shaded area. Never keep them for any length of time; in fact there is no point in retaining them at all unless they are to be weighed or photographed at the end of the fishing session.

Larger fish like carp, tench and pike are best retained in keepsacks where they lie quietly.

Never throw a fish into a net, but gently place it inside using wet hands.

When returning fish, gently gather up the net until the area occupied by the fish is reached; place the mouth of the net underwater and allow the fish to swim off.

A large fish should be held with both hands underwater in an upright position until it swims away.

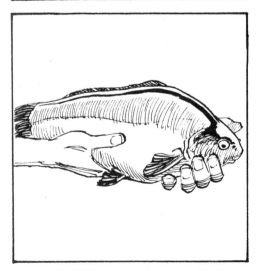

keepsack

Accessories

Keepnet

This item should always be as large as you can afford. Never buy one less than 6ft 6in (200cm). 13ft (400cm) would not be too big if a good swim was located holding large fish. A long net is also more practical where the water is shallow near the bank.

All keepnets have a screw fitting to accommodate a bank stick. To stop the net collapsing in the water, it is a good policy to secure the bottom of the net with another bank stick.

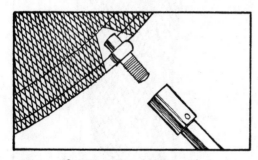

Screw fitting for bank stick.

Bank stick retaining bottom of net.

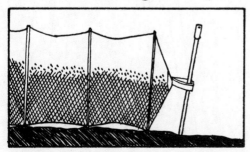

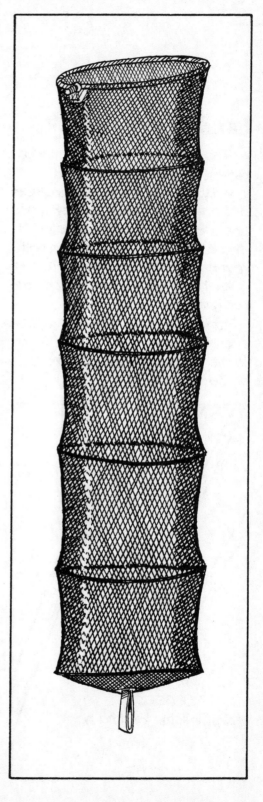

Landing net

The two basic shapes for landing net frames are circular and triangular. Materials used include alloy and fibreglass, both of which are used to make the handles. The same mesh is used for both keepnets and landing nets. This is a knotless nylon mesh, which does not harm the fish.

Frame sizes vary from the average-sized match net about 24in (60cm) to the specimen hunter's model of 36in (90cm)

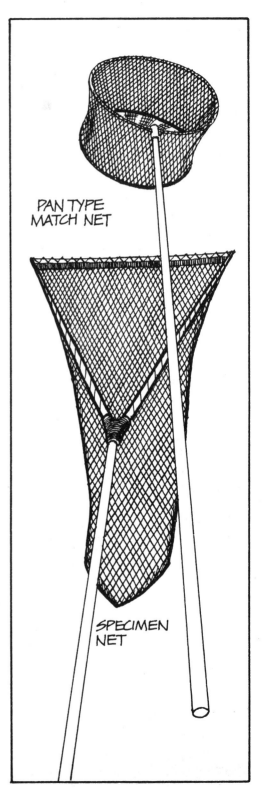

PAN TYPE
MATCH NET

SPECIMEN
NET

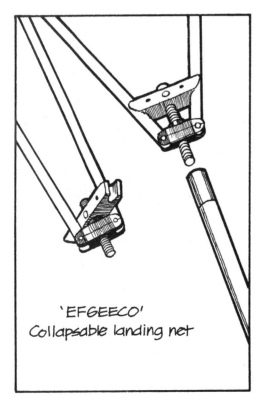

'EFGEECO'
Collapsable landing net

Baskets, boxes and seats

Traditional
cane basket

Fibreglass
tackle container

'Efgeeco' Tubular
framed tackle carrier

Although being superseded by more sophisticated material, the cane basket is still popular.

The fibreglass models are so well manufactured that they can actually be placed in several inches of water to provide a seat.

Metal-framed box-seats like the 'Efgeeco' model are excellent.

Where a lower profile is necessary, usually when carp fishing, a low, folding chair is ideal.

Catapult

If loose feed or groundbait balls have to be delivered at medium or long range a catapult is essential. It is advisable to have a spare length of elastic available in case of breakage.

If the catapult is fired with the handle in a vertical position, a painful rap on the knuckles will be experienced. To fire, tilt the handle over to one side.

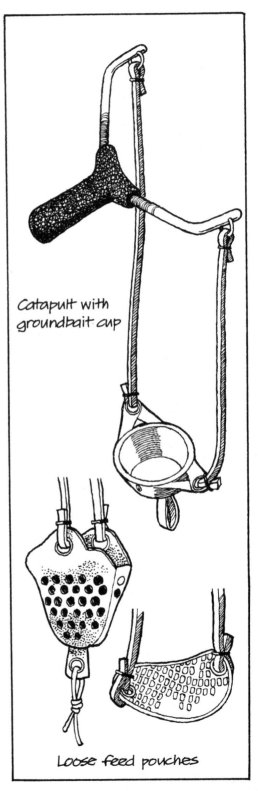

Catapult with groundbait cup

Loose feed pouches

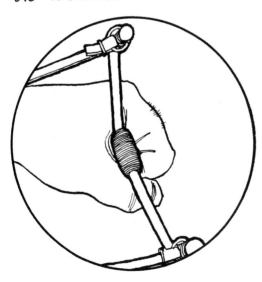

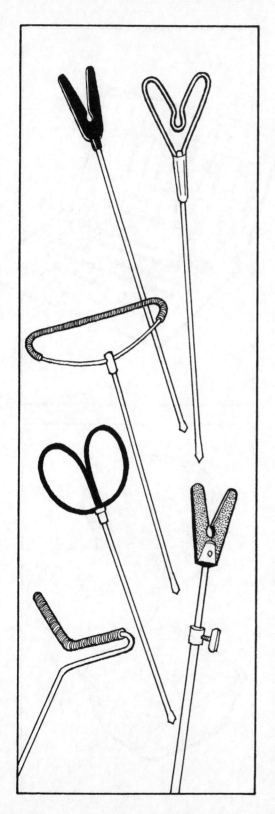

Rod-rests and bank sticks

Rod-rests come in a large variety of shapes and sizes but with one basic purpose, to support the rod while the angler waits for a bite. Many rests have an opening in the top to prevent the line being trapped by the rod; thus allowing line to be taken by a running fish after it has taken a legered bait.

Bank stick with screw fitting for taking detachable rod-rest.

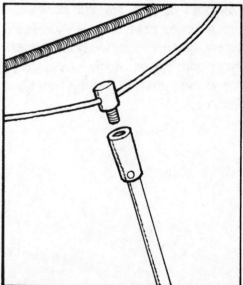

Float box

This item is invaluable if you want to keep your selection of floats in good condition. The floats are slotted into foam rubber strips, which hold them in place.

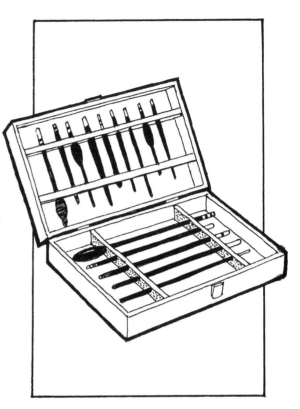

Bait container

Made from plastic with a snap-on lid. They are available in ½ pint, 1 pint and 2 pint sizes. They are most commonly used for maggots or casters, but can also be used to hold worms, sweetcorn, hemp, and most other baits. When transporting or storing maggots, make sure that the lid is securely fastened.

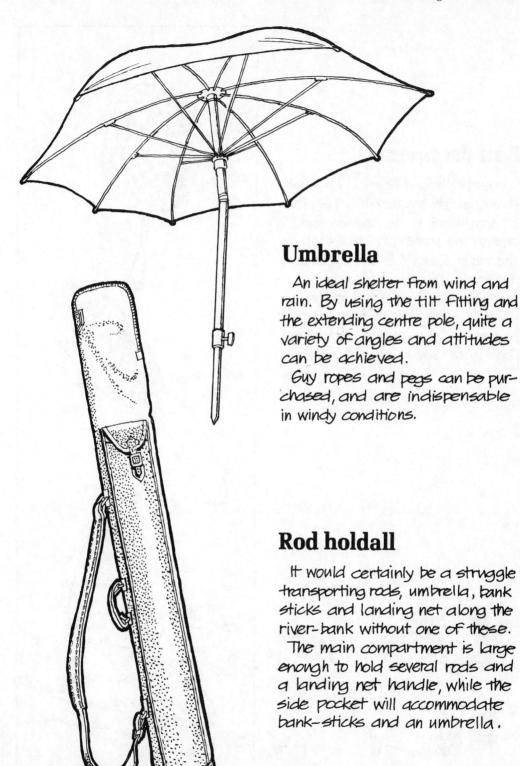

Umbrella

An ideal shelter from wind and rain. By using the tilt fitting and the extending centre pole, quite a variety of angles and attitudes can be achieved.

Guy ropes and pegs can be purchased, and are indispensable in windy conditions.

Rod holdall

It would certainly be a struggle transporting rods, umbrella, bank sticks and landing net along the river-bank without one of these.

The main compartment is large enough to hold several rods and a landing net handle, while the side pocket will accommodate bank-sticks and an umbrella.

Bait dropper

When fishing a fairly deep, fast swim, under the rod tip, this piece of equipment is the answer for presenting loose feed in exactly the right spot. It is attached to the line in the same way as the plummet and lowered into the swim. On making contact with the bottom, the flap opens and loose feed is released into the swim.

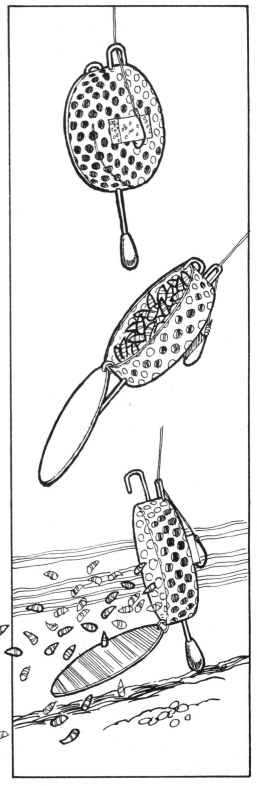

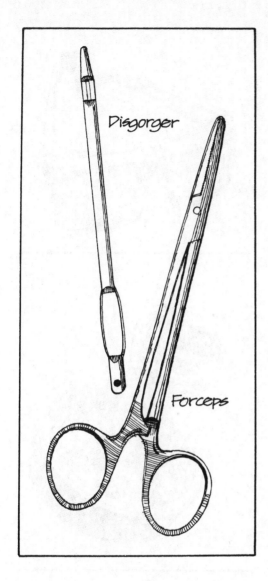

Disgorgers

Artery forceps are more suited to removing large hooks from the bigger species of fish such as carp, tench, chub etc.

The disgorger copes better with smaller hooks on fish like roach or dace.

Disgorgers with sharp points on the end are not recommended.

Reel case

A reel that is constantly stored loose in the bottom of a tackle container tends to collect bits of grit and dust, which can damage the internal mechanism.

A reel that is stored in a case when not in use is a clean reel, and therefore a more efficient reel.

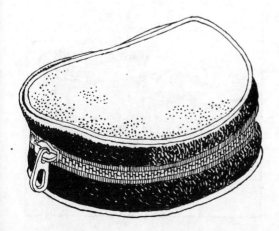

Polaroid glasses

These glasses eliminate glare, enabling the angler to see fish beneath the surface of the water.

Split shot container

Split shot can be purchased in individual plastic containers, or in segmented dispenser-type containers that hold a selection of different size shot. The shot is dispensed via a hole in the lid, which can be rotated to the required position.

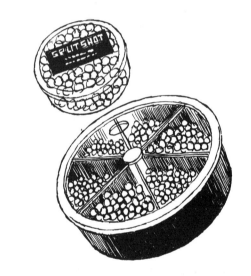

Spare spools

All fixed-spool reels have spools which are detachable, and easily changed in a matter of seconds. Be prepared for all eventualities by having a collection of spools, each loaded with different breaking strain line.

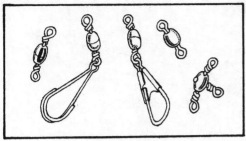

Swivels

Used for running leger links, and terminal tackle for pike fishing. Some swivels have a link attached (link swivels).

Float rubbers

Available in a large variety of sizes, either cut to size or in tube form, which allows the angler to tailor his own by cutting through the tube.

Nail clippers

The ideal tool for trimming the tag on the end of a knot.

Avon dial scales

Salter spring balance

Scales

A must for the angler who wants to keep a record of his catches. Weight capacity varies from just a few pounds up to 40lb (18 kg) plus.

How to cure a loose ferrule

Spigot ferrules, especially those on carbon fibre rods, tend to wear loose very quickly.

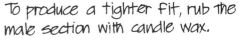

Spigot ferrule

A loose ferrule can be noticed immediately, because the male and female sections are touching one another when the rod is assembled.

To produce a tighter fit, rub the male section with candle wax.

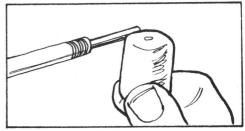

If the ferrule is very badly worn, more drastic measures will have to be taken.

A correctly fitting spigot ferrule should look like this.

Cut about ¼ in (6 mm) from the female section, then re-whip to provide support.

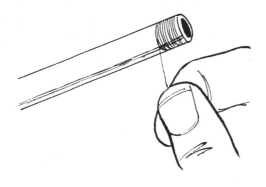

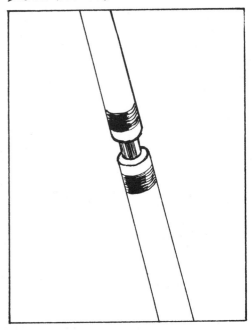

Whipping on a ring

Rods can be purchased in a half completed state, with just the handle and reel fitting secured to the blank. The rings are left to the angler. Ring positioning information is provided with the rod.

Start by securing one side of each ring to the rod. Sellotape is the ideal material for this.

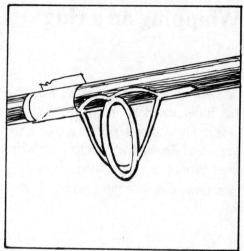

If single leg fuji rings are being used, a drop of super-glue will keep them in position, ready for whipping. Now is the time to make sure that all the rings are exactly in line.

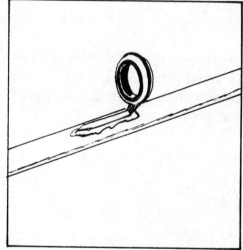

Starting at a point on the rod, just clear of the foot of the ring, wind the whipping thread back on itself for five or six turns, and cut off the tag end.

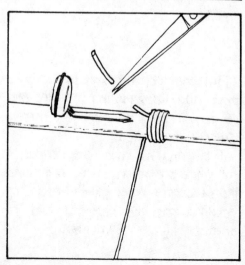

Whipping on a ring

Continue whipping, making sure that the turns are tight to one another. About five turns short of where you intend to finish, insert a loop of whipping thread or nylon monofilament, and continue whipping over this loop.

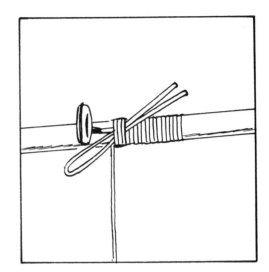

Making sure that a steady tension is being maintained, push the end of the whipping through the eye of the loop.

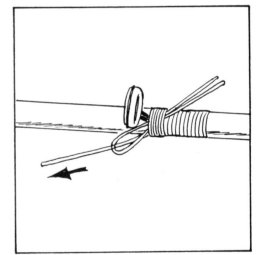

Pull the loop through the whipping, and keep pulling until the end of the whipping is completely through. Cut off the tag end.

If the ring has two feet, repeat the whole operation, after removing the sellotape. When all the rings are secured coat the whippings with two or three layers of varnish.

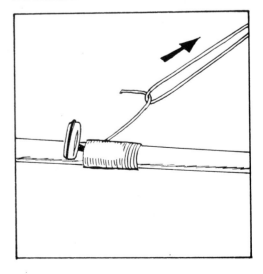

Knots

BLOOD KNOT: For joining two lengths of line of similar thickness. For joining lines of widely differing thickness, the tucked blood knot must be used.

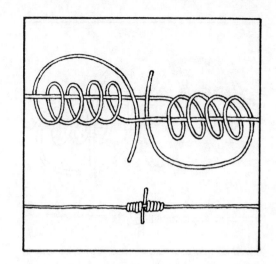

HALF-BLOOD KNOT: For attaching hooks, swivels and leads. This is a practical knot if the wire of the hook, swivel or lead is similar in diameter to the line being used. If the wire is a lot thicker than the line, then a tucked half-blood knot should be used.

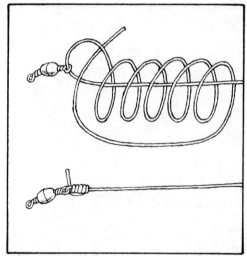

TUCKED HALF-BLOOD KNOT: A more efficient knot than the basic half-blood, and one that should always be employed if large fish are the quarry.

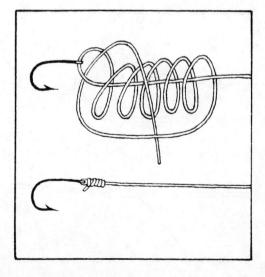

Knots

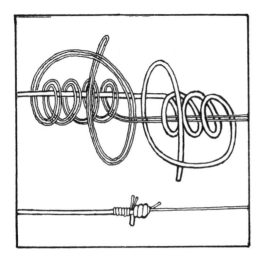

TUCKED FULL BLOOD KNOT: For joining line of widely differing thickness. The thinner line must be doubled within the tying area and taken around the thicker line twice as many times.

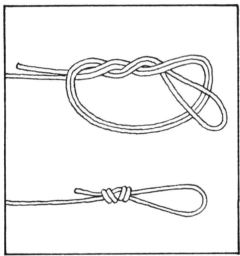

DOUBLE LOOP KNOT: A useful knot for joining a hook length to the main line. A loop is tied to the end of both the hook length and the main line.

Main line

Hook length

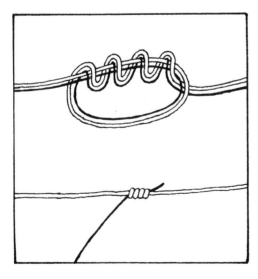

WATER KNOT: An excellent knot for attaching a leader, or a paternoster or leger link.

Knots

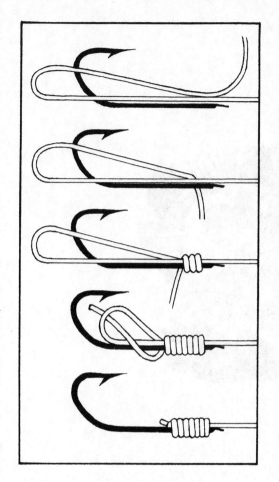

SPADE-END KNOT: Spade-end hooks can be purchased already tied to nylon. However, more and more anglers today are tying their own; shop-bought ones have a nasty habit of coming adrift just at the wrong moment. If you must purchase yours from a tackle shop, check every one of the batch.

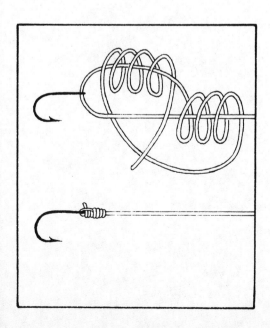

GRINNER KNOT: This knot is equally as good, if not better, than the tucked half blood knot. It just will not come adrift.

Always moisten the line with saliva before tightening any knot. Never jerk the line tight. A firm steady pull is sufficient. Leave about 1/32 in.(1 mm) of tag protruding from the finished knot.

FLYFISHING
FOR TROUT

Introduction

Fly fishing for trout is rightly regarded as the most subtle of the angling disciplines, and during the last two decades it has enjoyed a tremendous growth in popularity.

In the 1960s, a government decree mandated the water authorities to open their storage reservoirs to the public, thus greatly increasing the availability of good-quality trout fishing. From that moment, the boom in trout fishing gained momentum, and today it has become a highly valued recreational activity among many of this country's three million anglers. Indeed, increasing numbers of coarse and sea anglers gravitate to the reservoirs at the beginning of each season, to add fly fishing to their repertoire of fishing skills, and to have a change from their usual sport.

Whether you are a complete newcomer to fishing, or an experienced angler, it is essential, if you are to be a successful fly fisherman, that you are able to cast properly. In addition, a good casting style will enable you to fish with precision throughout a long day without becoming tired.

It is all too easy to fall into the trap of spending a lot of money on tackle before learning to cast. This can be a complete waste, and can set back your casting ability, and therefore your success rate, for years.

Your first rod can influence your style of casting for life. If a bad habit once becomes established, it will develop into a subconscious reflex. Before you know it, you will have a flaw in your technique which may take yards off the distance at which you are able to present a fly. And all the time, you remain blissfully unaware that this is happening.

In order to cast properly, you must be using the rod that is best suited to you, and the best place to get advice on casting and tackle is at one of the many professional casting schools that now exist. No matter how well intentioned your friend is when he offers to teach you, go to a good casting school as early on as you can, and certainly before you splash out hard cash on tackle. See what the professional is using, ask his advice, try the different rods he will have available; this is all part of what you are paying for.

Carbon fibre rods have now become so cheap that when you do buy a rod, you would be well advised to go straight to this space-age material. The rod should preferably be over 9 ft (2.75 m) in length. It is more difficult to cast a short rod than a longer one, so don't buy a shorter rod in the mistaken belief that it will be easier to use. But in any event, and it bears repeating, go to a professional school and get some advice.

There is another important point about tackle that I should like to make, and it concerns fly lines. Hard-won, practical experience has proved that your choice of fly line makes all the difference between a blank day and a full bag.

A good-quality line matched to the casting power of your rod is vital to good casting. However, it is the way in which that line behaves in the water that will determine whether or not you catch your quota of fish. And before anyone gets the wrong idea, the most expensive line, in my opinion, is not always the best.

You should walk the bank of your local reservoir or river, observing what tackle the majority of fishermen are using. Is it a floating line or one that sinks? What colour line is most used? Have a natter with anglers who are resting. However, don't, whatever you do, interrupt someone who may be chasing a fish. Most anglers are polite, but in such circumstances you may suffer some verbal indignities (see the section on bankside etiquette). Ask the angler what number line he thinks is best, what make, what rod is he using, and so on. It is also a good idea to join the local angling club, as you can then ask other members for advice. When anglers have been sufficiently 'lubricated' you can learn a lot from them; in addition, you will probably be treated to many entertaining half-truths that have been stretched further than they have any right to be.

Another advantage to joining a club is that during the winter months it will probably run a fly-tying class. Your local adult education centre may also run one, and it is well worth the effort to attend. Not only will tying your own flies save you money, but also the experience of landing a good fish on a fly which you have tied yourself is one of the most satisfying aspects of fly fishing. At first you will be tempted to try your hand at all sorts of wonderfully fluffy, highly-coloured lures, but over the years it is the simple, easily-tied flies which have endured and caught fish for generations of fly fishermen.

Make sure, when you step forth onto the bank for the first time, that your fly wallet is well stocked with classically simple flies, such as the legendary Black and Peacock spider, stick fly, worm fly, sedge pupa, and a few simply-tied lures, such as the Sweeny Todd, Black lure and Appetiser. These will be sufficient to catch fish under most conditions. Indeed a few of the very best fly fishermen rarely use more than half a dozen patterns right through the season, and catch just as many fish as any of us: a classic example of the rule which applies to all forms of fishing, 'Keep it simple and straightforward'.

When the author, Tony Whieldon, asked me to write this introduction to his book, I was both honoured and a little horrified at the task, because I know him to be a very able fly fisherman. What he has done in this book, as well as to demonstrate his superb draughtsmanship, is to show you his down-to-earth grasp of the information you need to know to catch trout, and I know he will join with me in wishing you 'Tight Lines'.

Russ Symons,
Plymouth, Devon.

Rods

Modern fly rods are man-ufactured in glass fibre, carbon fibre and boron. Carbon rods are always recognizable by their slim butt area just in front of the handle. The slimness belies their power for they are quite capable of throwing a line 40 yds (35 m) or more.

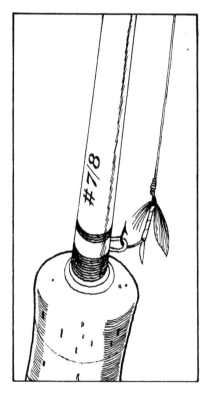

Just above the handle, on the rod itself, a number will show the manufacturer's rec-ommended line size for use with the rod.

In this instance a size 7 or 8 line would be suitable.

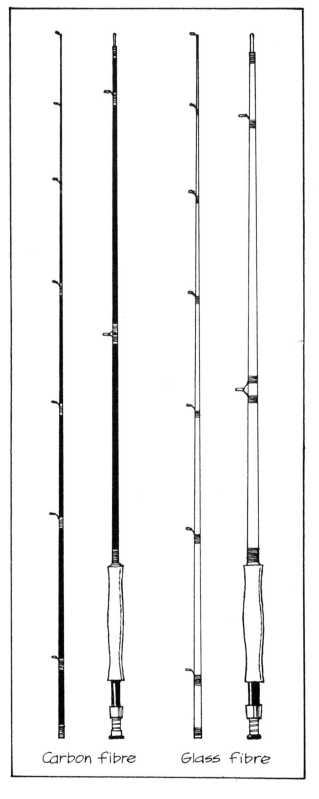

Carbon fibre   Glass fibre

Reels

Single action

SINGLE ACTION

As the original function of the fly reel is to store line in a con- venient package, this reel with its uncluttered design is the one used and favoured by the major- ity of fly fishermen.

Multiplier

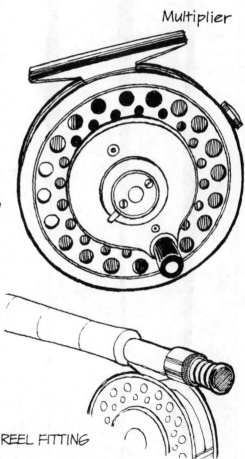

MULTIPLIER

For extra-fast line retrieve this reel excels. If you prefer this design, as many do, frequent lubrication will prolong its efficiency.

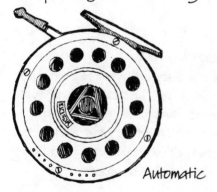

Automatic

AUTOMATIC

This reel strips line back on to the spool very fast, with the aid of a spring mechanism. Simply press the lever to keep in touch with a fast moving fish which is heading towards you.

REEL FITTING

It is a matter of choice which way the reel is secured. Some anglers have the handle on the right side, while others prefer a left-handed wind.

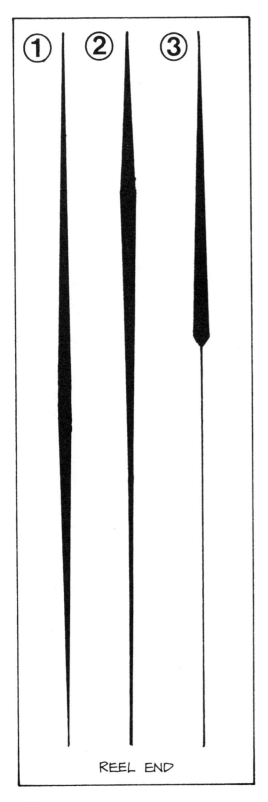

REEL END

Lines

① DOUBLE TAPER

The standard length for a fly line is 30yd (27·43m). For delicate presentation for close to medium-distance casting the DT is ideal. The economical advantage of this line is that it can be reversed, as each end is a mirror image of the other.

② WEIGHT FORWARD

Longer casts can be produced with this line, but with the drawback that when the line alights on the water surface quite a disturbance is created.

③ SHOOTING HEAD

This consists of what is virtually a double-taper line cut in half with an ample supply of much finer backing or shooting line tied to the rear end. It is capable of producing very long-distance casts.

Lines

FLOATING

This line sits on the surface of the water. It is used when fish are feeding on or near the surface. It can also be used in conjunction with a weighted nymph to seek out fish that are feeding close to the bottom.

SINK TIP

A floating line with about 10ft (3·05m) of sinking line at the forward end. Ideal for nymph fishing.

SLOW SINKING

This is a very useful line for searching different depths or for fishing a lure or a nymph at mid-water.

FAST SINKING

If the trout are feeding on or near the bottom in deep water, this is the line to use.

VERY FAST SINK, AND LEAD CORE

This line sinks very quickly and is invaluable for use in very deep water when the fishing is being done from a boat. Lead core is the ideal line for trolling a big lure behind a rowed boat.

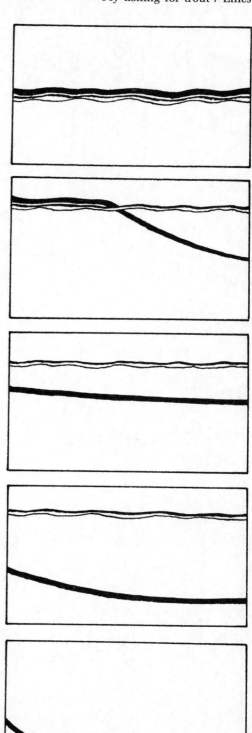

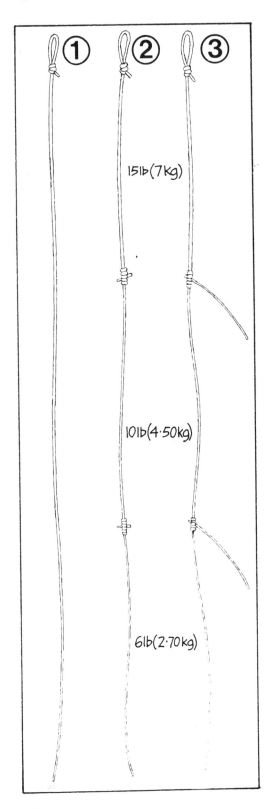

15lb (7kg)

10lb (4·50kg)

6lb (2·70kg)

Leaders

① KNOTLESS TAPER
For fine fly presentation these are the best, but they have one drawback; during the course of use, and after a number of flies have been changed, they obviously become shorter. This means that what started as a leader with, say, a 4lb (1·80kg) point will eventually become a leader with a 5lb (2·25kg) or a 6lb (2·70kg) point.

② KNOTTED TAPER
Many anglers today purchase small spools of nylon of different breaking strains and make their own. All that is then required to maintain the length is a new section of nylon at the point, which is connected to the rest of the leader via a blood knot.

③ TAPERED WITH TWO DROPPERS
This type of leader is mainly used for fishing loch-style from a drifting boat, although there is no reason why it should not be used from the bank.

The breaking strains shown are typical of what may be used when fishing a water where the trout run to around 10lb (4·50 kg) in weight. A finer section of, say, 4lb (1·80kg) may be added if the trout are smaller, or when using very small flies.

Line to leader

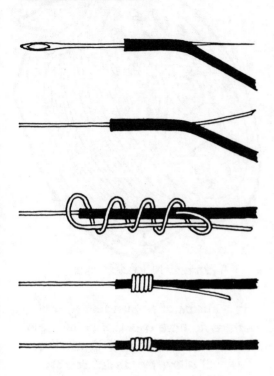

Line to backing

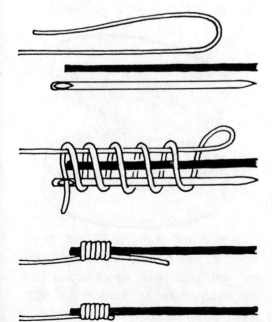

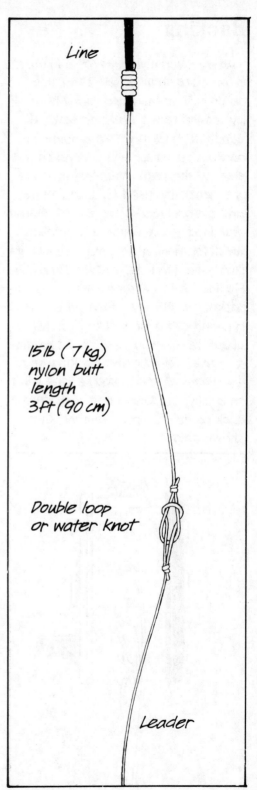

Line

15 lb (7 kg)
nylon butt
length
3 ft (90 cm)

Double loop
or water knot

Leader

Backing

As the overall length of a fly line is no more than 30yd (27m), it is necessary to increase the volume of line on the reel by adding several yards of backing. The amount of backing required will depend on the size of the reel. Wide-drum reels are generally used for lake fishing and obviously take more line than a standard spool, which is normally used for fishing on small to medium rivers. To find the answer, wind the fly line on to the spool, attach the backing to the line, then wind the backing on to the reel until it lies about ⅛in (4 mm) beneath the housing supports. Remove the backing and line from the reel, reverse, and wind on again, backing first. Attach the backing to the spool with the knot shown below.

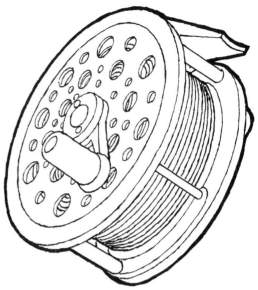

A correctly loaded reel

It is customary, when fishing still-waters, to have a selection of reels, each loaded with a different line. This will allow the angler to cope with the varied conditions and fish behaviour encountered on lakes.

When fishing on running water, a floating line is usually sufficient.

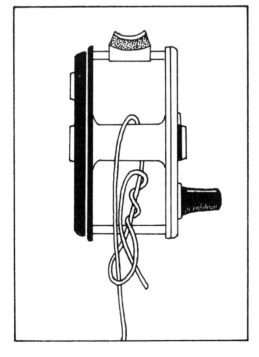

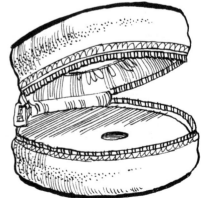

Look after your reels and they won't let you down. Reel cases keep out grit and dust which could harm the mechanism of the reel and the coating of the line.

Fly hooks

SPROAT hooks with a turned-down eye are probably the most ideally suited hook for the traditional wet fly patterns.

SPROAT hooks with a turned-up eye are used for dry flies, although some anglers prefer dry flies tied on the down-eyed hook.

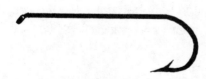

Lures, and most nymphs are tied on long shanked hooks with a turned-down eye.

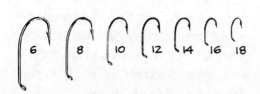

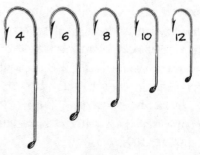

Artificial flies

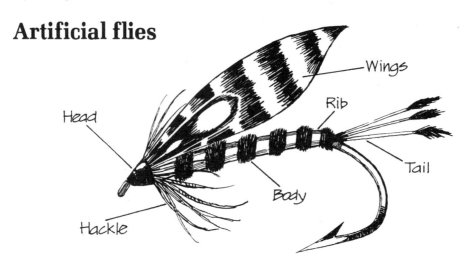

Head

Wings

Rib

Tail

Body

Hackle

DRY FLIES

Used when fish are taking insects from the surface. Equally effective on river and lake. Most dry flies are tied with the purpose of imitating, as closely as possible, a particular species of insect.

WET FLIES

Some of the traditional wet fly patterns bear some resemblance to aquatic life, but on the whole they are bright and flashy. The smaller, hackled wet flies used by the river angler for upstream fishing are, on the other hand, most life-like.

LURES

These probably account for more stillwater trout than all the other types combined, mainly because of their more widespread use. Colours used in their construction are as varied as the spectrum. They represent small fish rather than aquatic insect life.

NYMPHS

Mostly fished in conjunction with a floating line. Some patterns are weighted by the inclusion of lead wire beneath the body material. Of all the artificials, these are the most life-like. Patterns vary from the very small buzzer pupae up to the large damselfly nymphs.

Mayflies

These artificials represent the largest of the British mayflies, *Ephemera danica*, which appears on rivers and lakes during May, June or July.

Fan-winged Mayfly

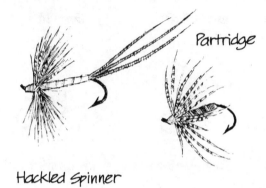

Partridge

Hackled Spinner

Hackle-point Spent Spinner

Popper lure

Anything less like a fly is hard to imagine, but this cork headed creation can be cast well enough with orthodox fly gear, and accounts for many good trout.

Use in conjunction with a floating line and retrieve with long steady pulls, across the water surface.

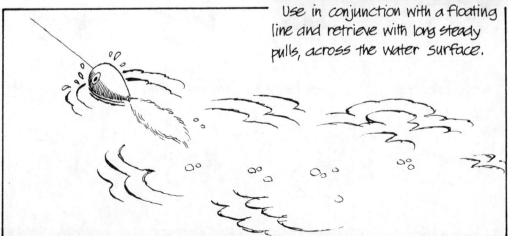

Dry flies

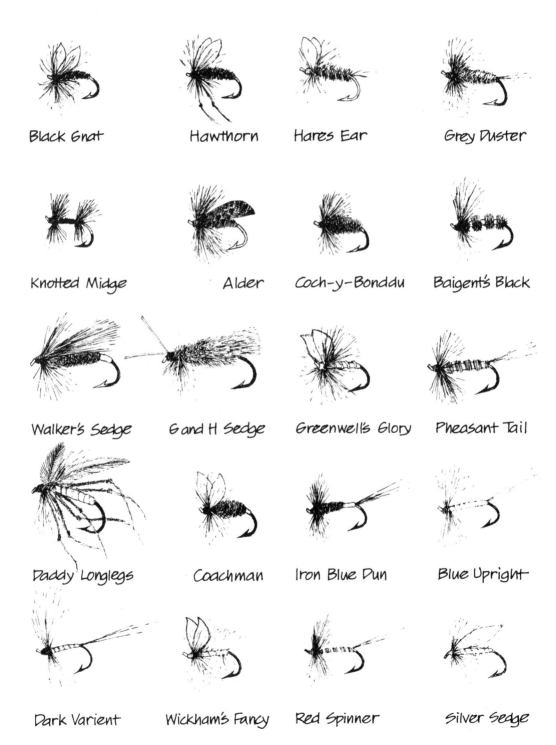

Black Gnat

Hawthorn

Hares Ear

Grey Duster

Knotted Midge

Alder

Coch-y-Bonddu

Baigent's Black

Walker's Sedge

G and H Sedge

Greenwell's Glory

Pheasant Tail

Daddy Longlegs

Coachman

Iron Blue Dun

Blue Upright

Dark Varient

Wickham's Fancy

Red Spinner

Silver Sedge

Wet flies

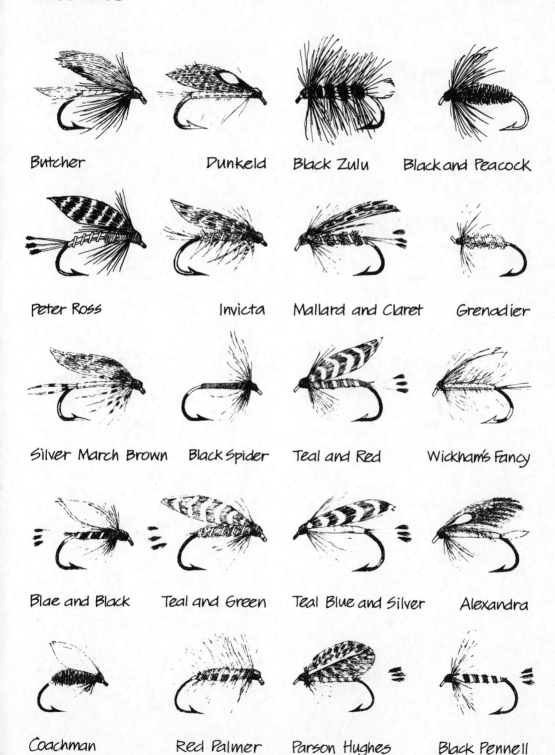

Butcher   Dunkeld   Black Zulu   Black and Peacock

Peter Ross   Invicta   Mallard and Claret   Grenadier

Silver March Brown   Black Spider   Teal and Red   Wickham's Fancy

Blae and Black   Teal and Green   Teal Blue and Silver   Alexandra

Coachman   Red Palmer   Parson Hughes   Black Pennell

Lures

Ace of Spades

Appetizer

Missionary

Jack Frost

Muddler Minnow

Church Fry

Baby Doll

Polystickle

Sweeny Todd

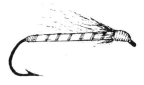

Whisky Fly

Lures

Worm Fly

Black and Orange Marabou

Badger Lure

Black Lure

Dog Nobbler

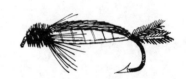

Jersey Herd

Perch Fry

Undertaker

Matuka

Viva

Nymphs

Amber Nymphs

MayFly Nymph

Damselfly Nymph

Pheasant Tail Nymph

Damsel Wiggle Nymph

Stick Fly

Collyer's Nymph

Montana Stone

Persuader

Brown Caddis

Nymphs and pupae

Midge Pupae

Footballer

Leaded Shrimp

Chompers

Corixa

Corixa (Plastazote)

Longhorns

Iven's Nymph

PVC Nymph

Sedge Pupae

Sawyer's Pheasant Tail Nymph

Bloodworm

Silver Nymph

Alder Larva

Cove's Pheasant Tail

Casting a fly

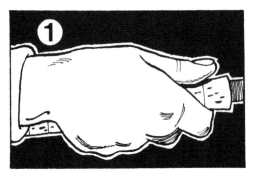

Hold the rod with the thumb on top of the handle....

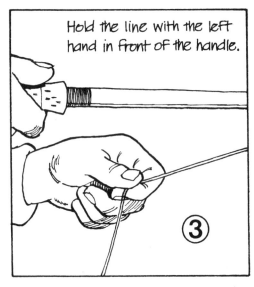

Hold the line with the left hand in front of the handle.

.... then pull enough line from the reel to provide enough weight to get the rod working properly.

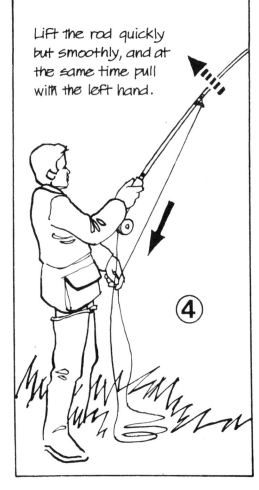

Lift the rod quickly but smoothly, and at the same time pull with the left hand.

Casting a fly

⑤ Stop the rod here. A common fault with many beginners is to let the rod fall back well beyond this point.

Pause in this position and let the line straighten out to the rear. If it helps, watch the line in the air.

⑥

⑦ Drive the rod forward....

.... and as the line unfurls over the water, release the line from the left hand, the 'shoot'!

⑧

Fishing a floating line

When the fish are active up in the surface area, and especially if you can see insects being blown on to the water surface, and being taken by the fish, it is worth using a dry fly.

Before the fly is cast, it should be 'dunked' in a bottle of floatant.

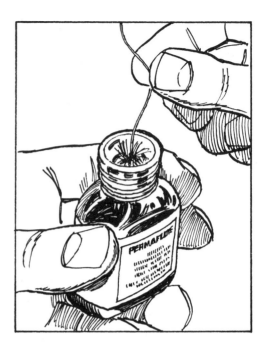

Dragging the fly across the surface in short erratic jerks will often produce a response.

A floating line can also be used to fish a nymph on or very near the bottom. In this case the leader will have to be longer than usual, (15ft (4.55m), and the nymph will need a weighted body (leaded nymph).

Whenever nymphs are being used, it is advisable to give the leader a wipe with 'leader sink'; a good substitute is washing-up liquid.

Fishing a floating line

Sometimes a trout will be seen leaving a trail of rings as it cruises just beneath the surface, sucking down insects which lie in its path. By logical deduction, it is possible to place your offering accurately ahead of the fish.

Next estimated rise

Present Fly here

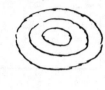
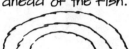

As nymphs or pupae rise to the surface to hatch, they are often intercepted by the fish before they reach the surface. This activity is perceptible only to the keenest eye. Binoculars are a great help when trout are feeding like this.

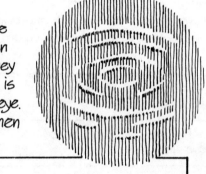

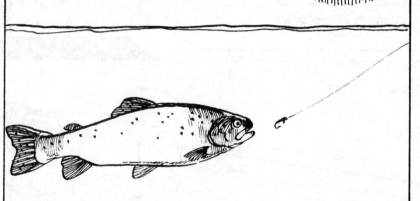

After the cast, pause awhile to let your nymph sink well beneath the surface, then retrieve line very slowly, pausing occasionally to keep the nymph about 12 in (30 cm) under the surface film.

125

Fishing a sinking line

Of the different types of sinking line the very slow sinker is the most versatile. It can be used to over—come a cross-wind problem, or to fish a nymph or lure in the upper layers of water, or over weedbeds and underwater snags.

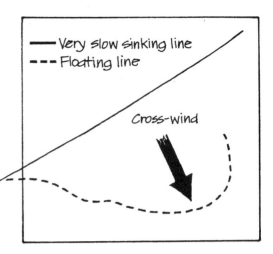

——— Very slow sinking line
- - - Floating line

Cross-wind

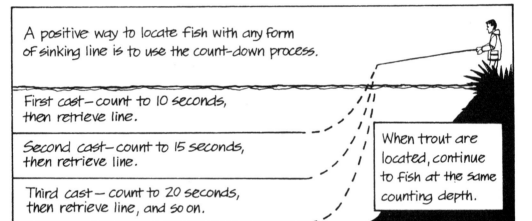

A positive way to locate fish with any form of sinking line is to use the count-down process.

First cast – count to 10 seconds, then retrieve line.

Second cast – count to 15 seconds, then retrieve line.

Third cast – count to 20 seconds, then retrieve line, and so on.

When trout are located, continue to fish at the same counting depth.

The way to retrieve a lure

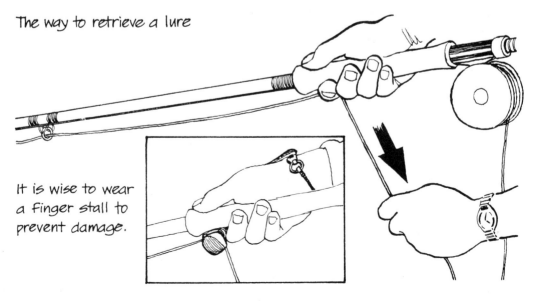

It is wise to wear a finger stall to prevent damage.

Fishing a sinking line

Although the very slow-sinking line is versatile it would not be practical to use it exclusively, as it would take far too long to sink to fish that were lying well down in very deep water.

When searching for fish in these deeper places use a fast, or very fast sinking line.

When retrieving a lure, especially quickly, it is important to hold the rod correctly in relation to the line. Some trout will take a lure in a very savage manner. It is therefore best to hold the rod at an angle to the line, in order to cushion the shock of a taking trout.

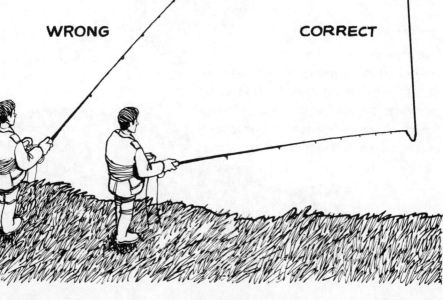

WRONG

CORRECT

Species

BROWN TROUT (Salmo trutta fario)

This trout is indigenous to Great Britain and Europe, and is found wherever the water has a high oxygen content, from the acid streams of high ground to the more alkaline waters of lower ground. Acid-water trout seldom grow to any great size, unless they have an unusually rich food supply.

RAINBOW TROUT (Salmo gairdneri)

Introduced to Europe and Britain in the 1880s, it is used extensively to stock man-made fisheries, but does not breed, except in a few places where the conditions are exactly suitable. Distinguishable by the magenta stripe along the flank.

AMERICAN BROOK TROUT
(Salvelinus fontinalis)

This fish is more a char than a trout but can be cross-bred with both the brown and the rainbow trout. A brook/brown trout cross is known as a 'tiger trout'.

Cannibal trout

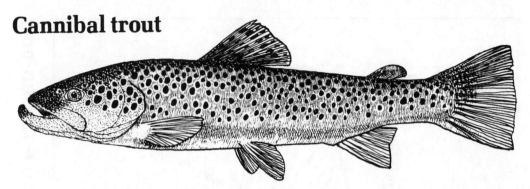

Old male trout very seldom bother to feed on surface-borne insect life, except, perhaps, when a heavy hatch of *Ephemera danica* is taking place.

They adopt, instead, a diet consisting of small coarse fish and trout. The nomenclator is very apt, for they can be as rapacious as any pike.

Ghost Swift

These predatory trout can be caught on lures. The perch-fry streamer is probably the best bet. At dusk and during the night they often swim near the surface, and can be caught on an imitation ghost-swift moth.

129

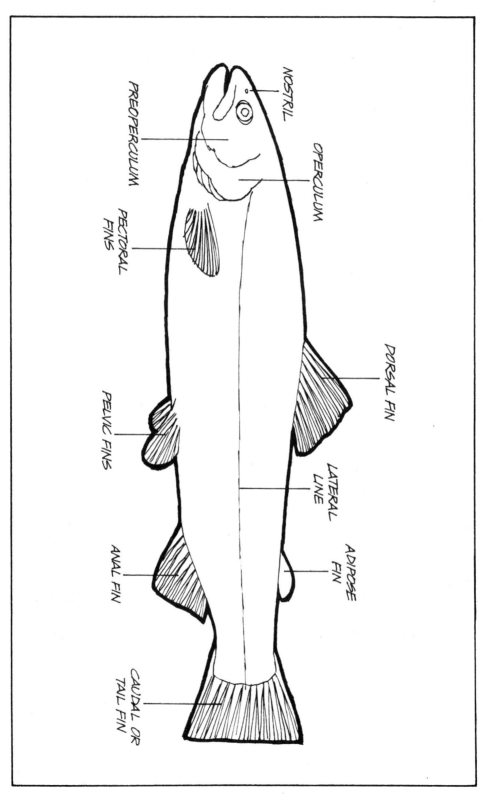

EPHEMEROPTERA (Mayflies)

The trout's diet

Members of this group of insects all have upright wings and two or three long tails. There are four stages in the metamorphosis: egg, nymph, sub-imago and imago. Fishermen refer to the sub-imago as the 'dun', and to the imago as the 'spinner'.

At the surface the 'dun' emerges from the nymphal skin.

The 'spinner' then emerges from the 'dun'.

After mating, the eggs are deposited into the water, and both male and female fall to the water surface as 'spent spinners'.

Nymphs are also taken by trout as they swim towards the surface.

These dead and dying flies are easy prey for trout.

After hatching from the egg the nymph lives and feeds on the bottom. Some are eaten at this stage by foraging trout.

131

The trout's diet

Other groups of insects go through a similar sort of development as the Ephemeroptera. All the stages shown below form part of the trout's diet.

Adult

DIPTERA: In this group, the midges (Chironomids) are of most interest to trout.

Pupa

Larva (bloodworm)

TRICHOPTERA: This group includes the caddis or sedge flies.

Caddis larvae in cases

Pupa

 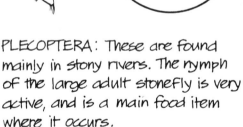

Adult

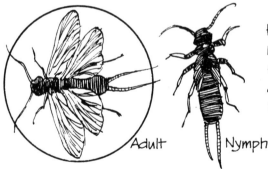

Adult   Nymph

PLECOPTERA: These are found mainly in stony rivers. The nymph of the large adult stonefly is very active, and is a main food item where it occurs.

ZYGOPTERA: Adult damselflies are occasionally taken by trout, but the nymph is a main food item.

Nymph

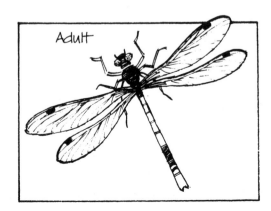

Adult

The trout's diet

Many other species of non-aquatic insects form part of the trout's diet. These are blown on to the surface of the water by the wind. Here are the two most commonly encountered.

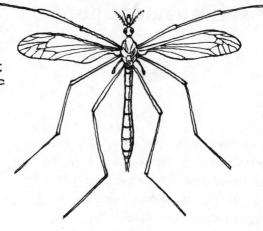

Hawthorn Fly

Crane Fly

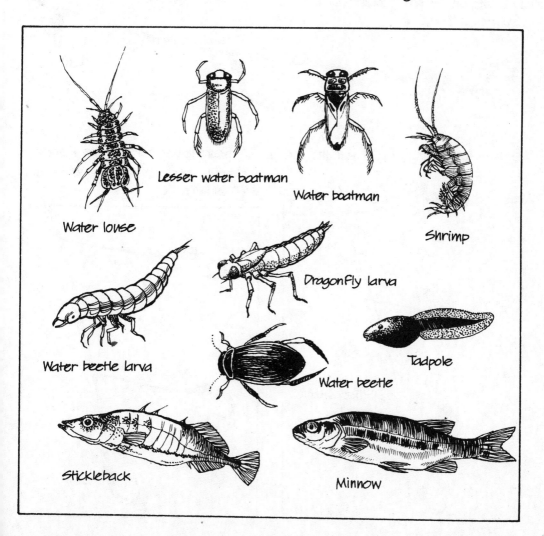

Water louse

Lesser water boatman

Water boatman

Shrimp

Water beetle larva

Dragonfly larva

Water beetle

Tadpole

Stickleback

Minnow

133

Fishing a midge pupa

This artificial is meant to represent the pupae of chironomidae (midges) which hang in the surface film before their final metamorphosis into the adult midge (buzzer).

To ensure that the artificial hangs stationary in the surface film, the leader should be greased so that it floats. Mount two or three on the leader, each one stopped by a blood knot. Tie a sedge, well treated with floatant, on the point to act as an additional buoy.

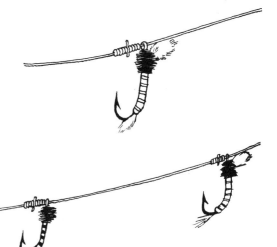

Set-up for fishing pupae near the bottom.

Strike when the sedge disappears.

Midge pupae can also be fished in the traditional style, and retrieved very slowly.

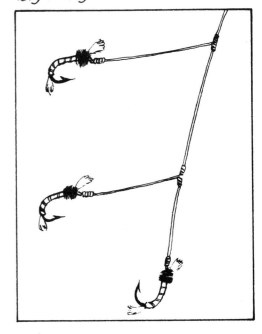

Fishing a sedge pupa

This pattern is a general representation of the many different sedge pupae found in most still-waters. During the summer months, the natural swims to the surface, or to the shore, in order to undergo the final transformation and become an adult sedge fly.

The artificial can be fished at mid-water, or near the bottom with a sinking line ....

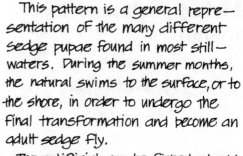

.... or just under the surface with a floating, sink-tip, or very slow-sinking line.

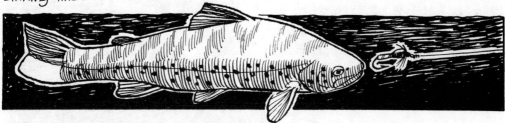

Retrieve the pupa at a medium pace, with long steady pulls, and a pause here and there.

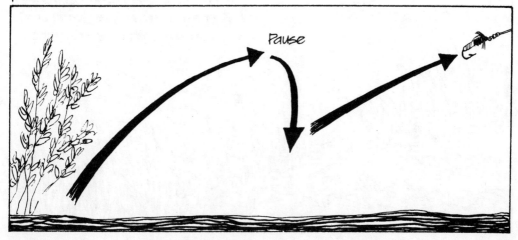

Pause

135

Fishing a damselfly nymph

During the early part of the season this pattern can be fished, very slowly, along the bottom. Shallower bays, where weed is prolific during the summer, are the most likely areas to attract the natural nymphs, as they feed largely on decaying vegetable matter.

During the warmer months the nymphs are far more active and wriggle to the surface, whereupon they proceed to swim towards the shore or surface weed in order to hatch into adult damselflies. To simulate this activity, fish the artificial just under the surface with a fairly fast retrieve, on a floating line.

Where there are rushes or reeds, it is often more productive to cast and retrieve along the shoreline.

Fishing a daddy-long-legs

The crane fly or 'daddy-long-legs' is a familiar sight at the waterside from June onwards. They are often blown onto the water surface where they struggle in their attempts to become air-borne once more. Such a large insect presents a good mouthful to the trout, which respond avidly.

Cast the artificial to an area where trout activity is obvious on the surface, (the fly will need to be well 'dunked' in floatant), then just wait for a fish to find it.

When a take does occur, resist the temptation to strike, as the trout will often try to drown the fly first, before taking it in its mouth.

Wait until the line starts to run out, then lift the rod high to set the hook.

Drag a 'daddy-long-legs' through a heavy ripple, or waves, and the trout will often respond with a very positive take.

137

Fishing a corixa

This pattern imitates the lesser water-boatman which spends most of its life near the bed of the lake, but has to rise to the surface in order to replenish its air supply.

Two patterns have developed to represent this little bug. The leaded version, which can be fished via a floating or a sinking line close to the bottom...

... and the buoyant (plastazote) version, which has to be fished with a sinking line.

Cast the buoyant corixa and allow the line to sink – the corixa will float on or near the surface.

When the line is retrieved, the corixa will dive towards the bottom, imitating, in a very life-like manner, the action of a water-boatman as it swims back to base.

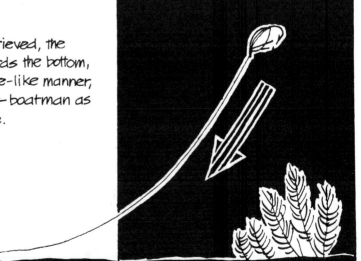

Fishing a leaded shrimp

This pattern represents the fresh-water shrimp, Gammarus; a resident of well-oxygenated water. They thrive in watercress, suggesting therefore that lakes fed by streams containing this plant would be ideal places to use this very effective little pattern.

A leaded shrimp is ideally suited for margin fishing in clear-water lakes. Let the shrimp sink to the bottom where trout are patrolling.

The combination of lead wire and the shape of the body results in the artificial adopting an inverted attitude, which simulates the natural in a very life-like manner.

When a trout approaches, inch the shrimp off the bottom in short jerks.

Lake fishing

Protective clothing is of vital importance to the angler who fishes the exposed banks of large still-water fisheries.

A waxed proofed cotton jacket complete with hood and storm collar will keep the elements at bay. Thigh waders will keep the legs warm and dry. Make sure that the jacket hangs well down over the top of the waders.

The tackle bag should be large and roomy to accommodate, apart from spare reels etc., the large fly box which is necessary to hold the comprehensive selection of flies and lures that is required for lake fishing.

Lake fishing from the bank

The expanse of an unfamiliar lake may pose a problem to a visiting angler, but if he applies his knowledge and experience of other lakes to this one, he will soon locate fish. For every lake, whether it is man-made or natural, has features in common with other lakes, as well as its own personal characteristics. Here are some places well worth attention.

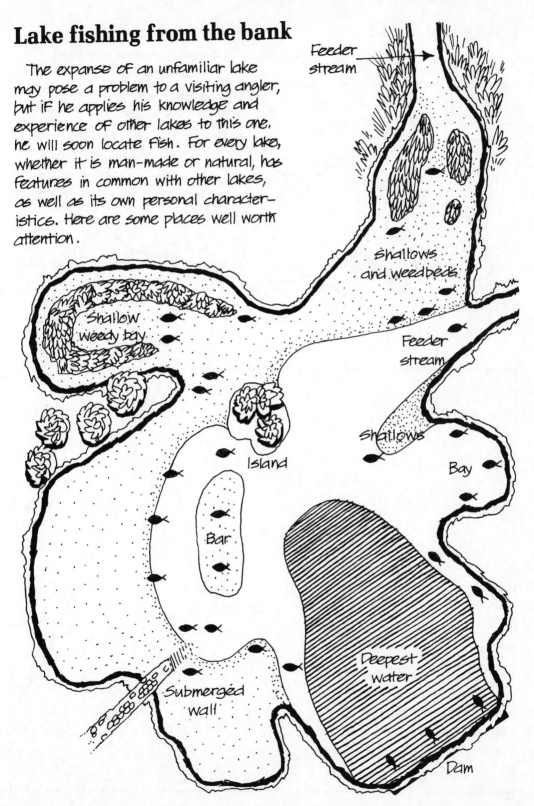

Feeder stream

Shallows and weedbeds

Shallow weedy bay

Feeder stream

Shallows

Island

Bay

Bar

Deepest water

Submerged wall

Dam

Using the wind

The wind can often be of assistance in the location of fish. Warm
winds from the south, and south-
west are best, both for fish and
fishermen.

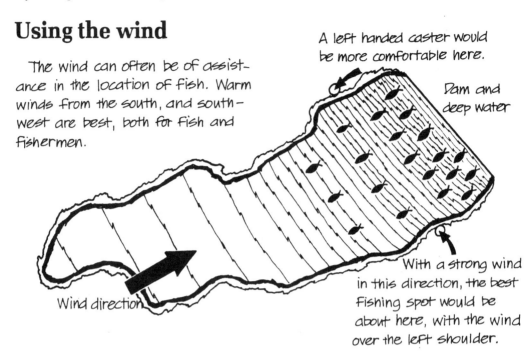

A left handed caster would
be more comfortable here.

Dam and
deep water

Wind direction

With a strong wind
in this direction, the best
fishing spot would be
about here, with the wind
over the left shoulder.

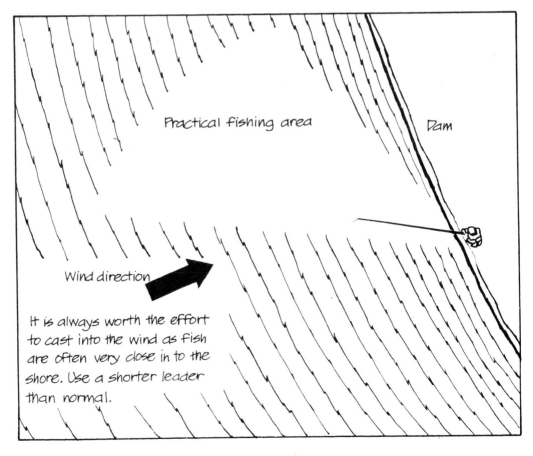

Practical fishing area

Dam

Wind direction

It is always worth the effort
to cast into the wind as fish
are often very close in to the
shore. Use a shorter leader
than normal.

Lake fishing from the bank

When fish are showing on the surface, they are usually feeding on
insects which have been blown on to
the water surface from the shore,
or on nymphs or pupae hanging in
the surface film.

If there are a number of fish
rising fairly close together, cast
among them and work the fly back
slowly in very short jerks.

Method of retrieving a small fly or
or nymph with a floating line.

143

Fishing a lure from the bank

Hungry, early-season trout will grab almost any lure that is cast into a lake. Some lakes at this time of year tend to carry a certain amount of colour, which demands the use of a high-visibility lure, such as a Jack Frost, Appetizer, Ace of Spades or Dog Nobbler.

As the season advances, however, the food supply is more abundant, and the trout become more selective. Nymphs and flies are then the main items of food, but where fish fry exist these are also taken, and it is possible to imitate them with a lure. The shallows of many lakes support a healthy population of sticklebacks, minnows and other small fry on which the trout feed.

High visibility lures

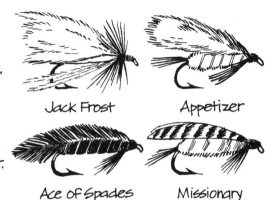

Jack Frost · Appetizer

Ace of Spades · Missionary

Fry imitators

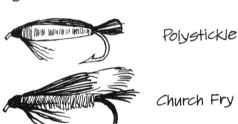
Polystickle

Church Fry

Jersey Herd

Sinfoil's Fry

Where fry activity is seen, cast a fry lure along the shore-line.

Fishing a lure from the bank

The Dog Nobbler is rather unusual inasmuch as it carries a whole split-shot as part of its dressing. It certainly does not represent anything in particular, but when drawn through the water it has a very stimulating action.

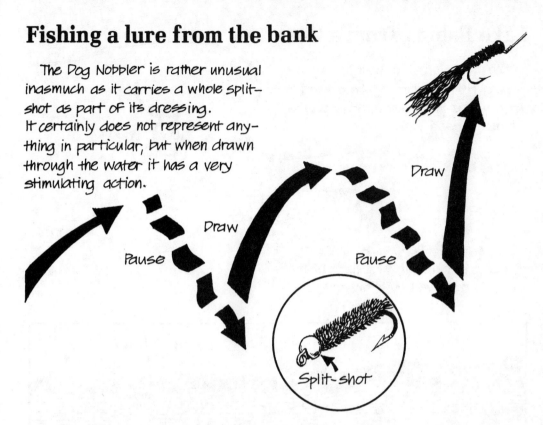

Split-shot

Another unique lure is the Muddler Minnow, which has the tendency to float, rather than sink like the Dog Nobbler. In medium-depth water it works better on a floating line; but in deep water, a fast-sinking line is more suitable if the fish are swimming deeper.

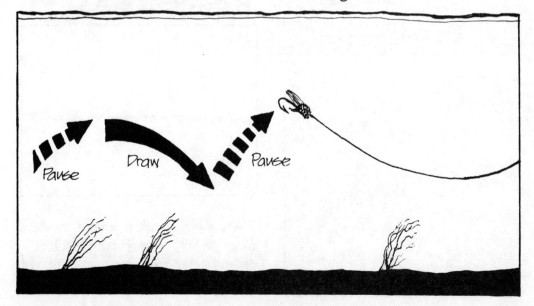

Lake fishing from a boat

The traditional loch style of fishing from a drifting boat is still very widely practised, and accounts for many good fish.

Bob Fly

Point fly

Middle dropper

The team of flies is cast ahead of the drifting boat on a fairly short line, and retrieved by lifting the rod.

A zulu is an ideal pattern to use as a bob fly, and if possible it should be made to dribble through the surface during the retrieve.

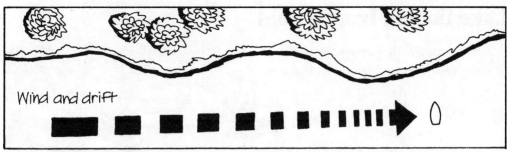

Wind and drift

The drift is usually performed along, and not too far out from, the shore-line. When the boat is drifting too quickly a drogue can be used to check its progress.

←Drift →

Suggested patterns and positions

POINT	MIDDLE DROPPER	BOB
Butcher	Invicta	Zulu
Dunkeld	Mallard and Claret	Invicta
Peter Ross	Silver March Brown	Red Palmer
Teal Blue and Silver	Teal and Red	Greenwells Glory
Alexandra	Wickhams Fancy	Black and Peacock Spider

Lake fishing from a boat

Casting a dry fly to rising trout is a delightful form of boat-fishing.

This is particularly effective when flies, especially hawthorn flies and crane flies, are being blown on to the lake from the shore.

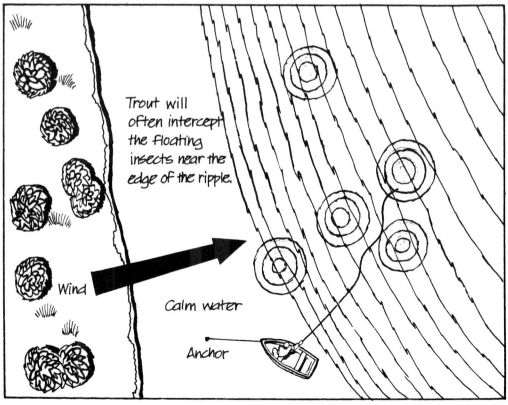

Trout will often intercept the floating insects near the edge of the ripple.

Wind

Calm water

Anchor

Dapping with a daddy-long-legs

Dapping with a natural daddy-long-legs has been a method of angling practised for many years, on some Irish and Scottish lochs.

Given the right conditions, this form of fishing can be applied to most stillwater fisheries. There is no need to use the natural insect either—an artificial 'daddy' works just as well.

The boat is allowed to drift before the wind, just as with the loch-style of wet fly fishing. The rod, however, needs to be as long as possible in order to present plenty of line to the wind.

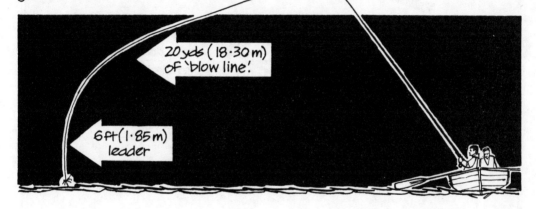

20 yds (18·30 m) of 'blow line'

6 ft (1·85 m) leader

Simply let the line blow out over the water, and attempt to keep the fly dancing in the waves.

With this method, an over-hasty strike will result in a missed fish. Wait until the trout has turned down with the fly in its mouth, then just tighten up.

Lure fishing from a boat is un-doubtably a very productive form of trout fishing. A single lure can be fished just beneath the surface, at mid-water, or on the bottom.

Lure fishing from a boat

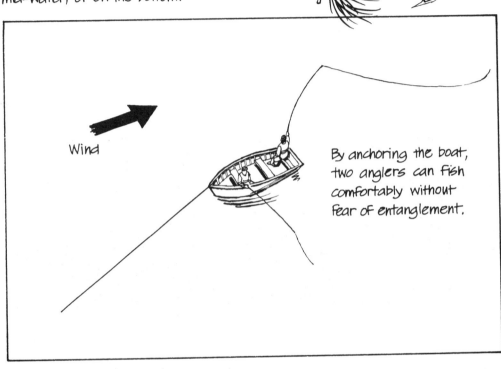

Wind

By anchoring the boat, two anglers can fish comfortably without fear of entanglement.

Expect a take at any time, even when the retrieve has almost finished. Some really vicious takes occur when the lure is close under the boat.

Trolling

This method involves trailing a lure about 30–40 yd (28–36 m) behind a rowing boat. A lead core line is used to keep the lure well down in the water. Lures used for this sort of fishing are usually of the tandem variety.

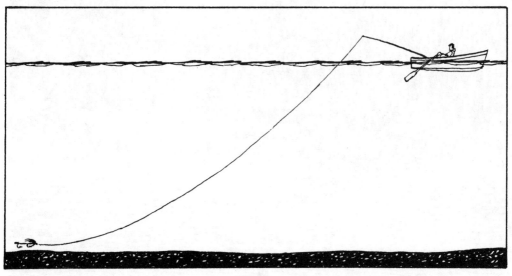

Trout caught with this method are generally larger than average.

151

River and stream fishing

Trout can be found in most rivers and streams where the water is clean. The trout of the fast rocky streams of the higher ground are usually small in comparison to the fish of the lowland rivers. Because of the turbulent nature of the rocky stream, wet fly fishing is the method most widely employed. On the lowland river, where the flow is more sedate, the dry fly is favoured.

Moorland stream

Lowland stream

River and stream fishing

There is no need for a heavy line when fishing a stream. No's. 4, 5 or 6 will be ideal. A light coloured line will show up far better in the shadows of overhanging foliage.

Other items needed will include; waders, strong tackle bag with a wide shoulder strap, collapsible landing net, priest, fly floatant, leader sink (if nymph fishing), scissors, spare leaders and a selection of flies.

River and stream fishing

The successful river fly-fisherman is the one who moves with stealth, and remains outside the trout's field of vision.

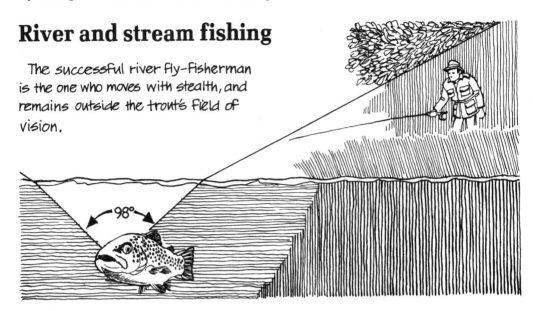

In very clear water, a trout lying near the river bed will have a larger field of vision than a trout lying near the surface.

It is obvious from the above diagram that the only blind spot is directly to the rear of the trout. Whenever possible, approach the fish from that direction; especially when fishing in a confined area such as is commonly encountered on small overgrown streams.

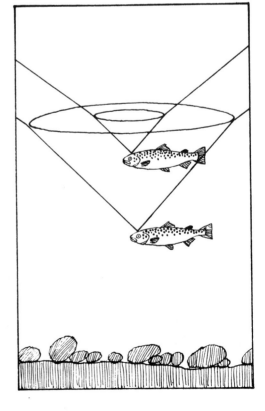

Drab clothing merges with the background, and aids concealment, even when the angler is in the trout's field of vision.

Olive-green, waxed cotton jackets, or army surplus combat jackets are ideal.

It is often necessary to wade, even on small streams. Again, olive-green is the best colour to choose for waders, and they should not have studs. A better grip may be provided by studs on some surfaces, but they produce such a clatter on stones and pebbles that the trout can detect the vibration yards away.

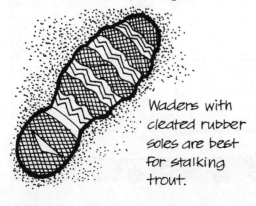

Waders with cleated rubber soles are best for stalking trout.

Concealment

The ideal position to be in, when wading a pool, is tucked away under the bank. For safety's sake, always tread very carefully; even small streams contain deep and sudden drop-offs into nasty holes. There is nothing as effective as a wader full of water for dampening the spirits.

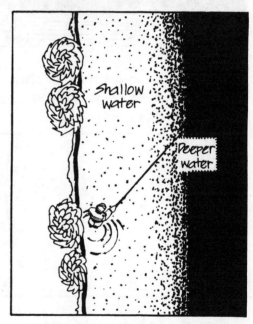

Shallow water

Deeper water

FIRM SILT OR SAND

The ideal material for wading on; muffles sound very efficiently.

ROCK

Cleated soles are silent on this, but it can be slippery.

PEBBLES

The worst base for stalking on. It is very noisy and sends shock waves right through a pool.

155

Fly presentation

When fishing in the confines of an overgrown stream the overhead cast is seldom practical. Instead, use the side cast.

The principal and timing of the side cast are the same as those of the overhead cast.

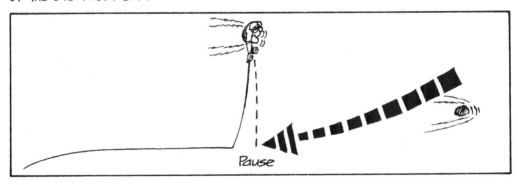

Pause

Work the line on an imaginary plane between overhanging foliage and the water surface.

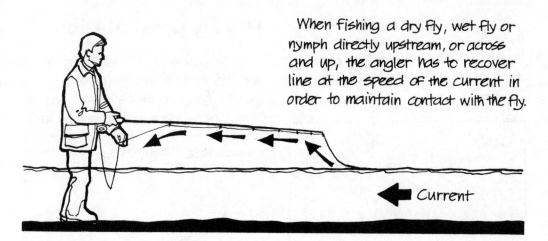

When fishing a dry fly, wet fly or nymph directly upstream, or across and up, the angler has to recover line at the speed of the current in order to maintain contact with the fly.

Current

When fishing from the bank on a small stream, with a short line on the water, the same effect can be achieved by moving the rod.

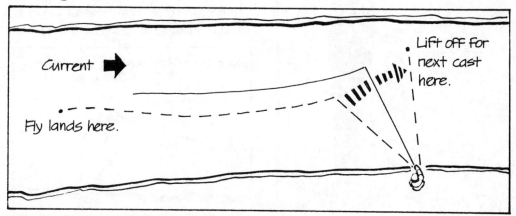

Current

Lift off for next cast here.

Fly lands here.

Presentation of a floating fly directly downstream.

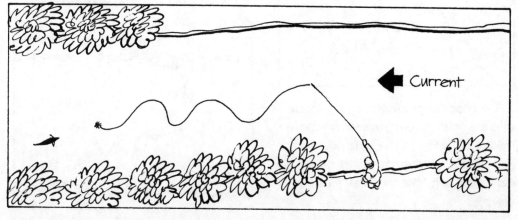

Current

Trout in a river always lie with their heads facing upstream, so it therefore makes sense to approach them from the rear, gradually working your way upstream.

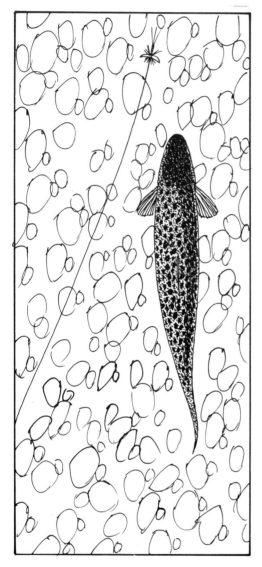

A correctly-presented fly should alight, gently, just ahead of the rising trout. If the fly lands too far ahead of the trout, the line may fall into the trout's field of vision.

Dry fly presentation

When you have to fish across the stream to the trout, you should have no problem as long as the flow is even from bank to bank.

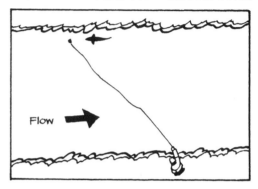

Flow

Unfortunately, conditions do not always present a perfect situation.

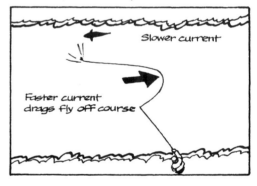

Slower current

Faster current drags fly off course

The remedy for this is to create some slack line.

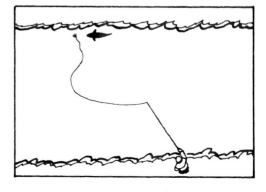

Dry fly presentation

When two or more trout are rising in close proximity to one another, care must be taken to select the fish in the correct order, to avoid scaring the other fish.

There are occasions when rises are few and far between, but this does not mean efforts with the dry fly will prove fruitless. Cover every likely-looking spot with a cast or two, and be prepared for a take just as if you had cast to a rising fish. Here are some places worth trying.

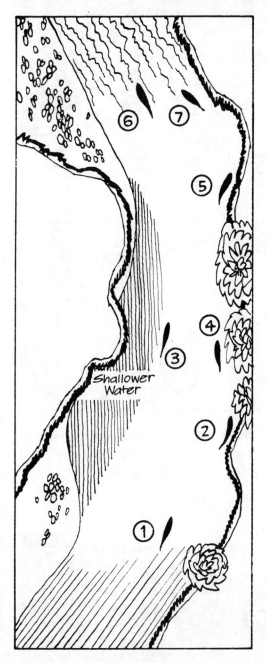

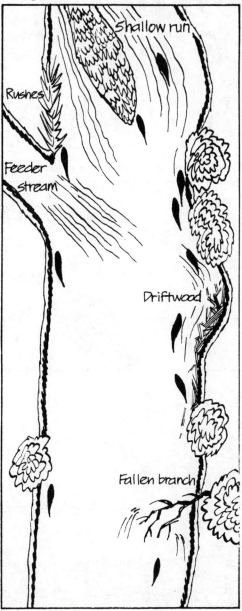

Upstream wet fly

Smaller, fast-flowing, overgrown streams are ideally suited to the upstream wet fly method.

Trout lies in a small rocky river

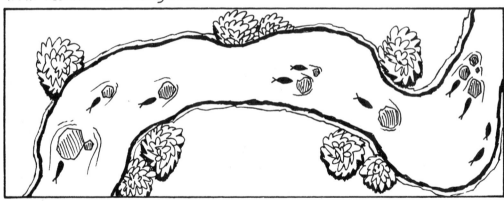

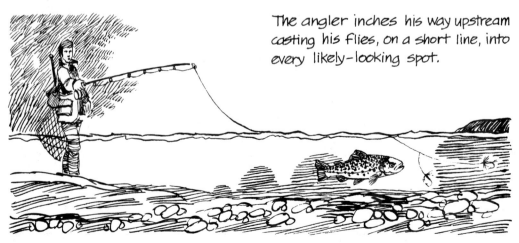

The angler inches his way upstream casting his flies, on a short line, into every likely-looking spot.

The downstream method

This method is practised with a team of, usually, three flies, similar to that used in the traditional loch method, but using smaller patterns. It is best employed on the larger, swiftly-flowing rocky rivers.

◀ Current

The flies are allowed to swing across the current in a wide arc.

The angler gradually works his way downstream, covering a lot of water with his flies in the process.

Pay special attention to the quieter water on the downstream side of large stones.

161

The more sedate flow of the lowland river is ideally suited to fishing a nymph. Nymph fishing comes into its own when the trout are not feeding on the imago, but are intercepting the nymph as it swims to the surface or is being carried along in the flow of the current. If trout are 'bulging' just beneath the surface, or are showing their tails, then this is the time to tie on a nymph.

Presenting a nymph in running water

The artificial nymph is fished singly and cast upstream; in fact, the whole procedure is like dry fly fishing, except that here the nymph is meant to sink as soon as it hits the water. In nymph fishing, the avoidance of drag is not important. Nymphs are free-swimming and the trout take them as they swim in all directions.

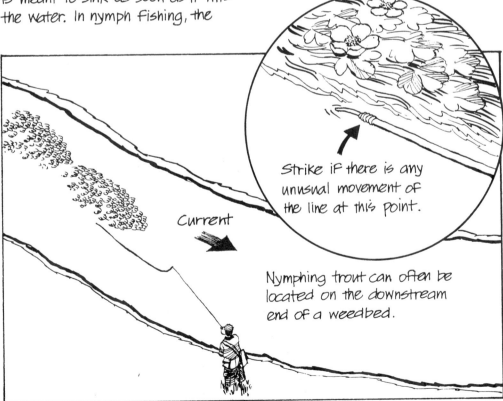

Current

Strike if there is any unusual movement of the line at this point.

Nymphing trout can often be located on the downstream end of a weedbed.

Small stream dapping

On many small streams bank-side foliage is so dense as to make ortho-dox fly presentation impossible. How-ever, the angler who uses a little init-iative and stealth, can extract trout that would make the locals gasp with astonishment.

The angler should walk slowly and quietly along the bank, or sit in a position which affords a reasonable view of the water. Eventually a trout will show itself by rising.

The angler should then take up a position directly over the fish. Conceal-ment and stealth are now even more important. The rod is poked through the foliage and the fly lowered until it touches the surface of the water. Some movement can be imparted to the fly by jiggling the rod-tip.

When the trout takes the fly, the rod-tip should be lowered before lifting into the fish.

A long-handled net is almost always necessary to extract trout from these confined places.

Ideal patterns for stream dapping.

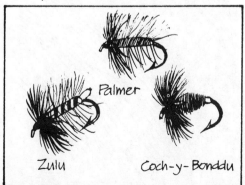

Palmer

Zulu

Coch-y-Bonddu

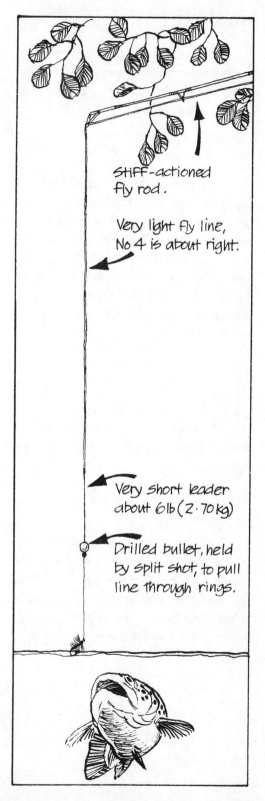

Stiff-actioned fly rod.

Very light fly line, No 4 is about right.

Very short leader about 6lb (2.70kg)

Drilled bullet, held by split shot, to pull line through rings.

Hooking

A trout taking a wet fly fished downstream in fast water will often hook itself. The angler feels the tug and the fish is on.

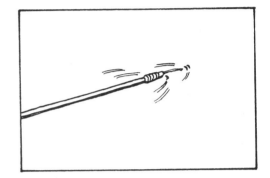

The take of a trout that has just accepted an upstream wet fly or a nymph is far more subtle. The best way to detect these invisible takes is to watch the point where the line joins the leader. When a take occurs the line will stop, or be drawn upstream. Then is the time to tighten on the fish.

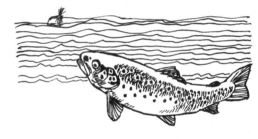

A small trout snatching at a dry fly in a fast stream needs to be struck very quickly, by flicking back the wrist.

Larger trout in slower, quieter water should be allowed to turn well down with the fly; in fact, it is often advisable to wait until the line starts to move forward. This is particularly important on the majority of still-waters.

Playing and landing

Once the hook is set, the rod-tip should be held well up. A small trout dashing around a pool in a moorland stream should prove no problem; the elasticity of the rod-tip will absorb its activity until it is ready for the net. Larger trout, however, will have to be given some line, but with a steady strain applied.

The rod-tip should be held well up.

Some anglers play a trout from the reel, while others prefer to control the fish via the line.

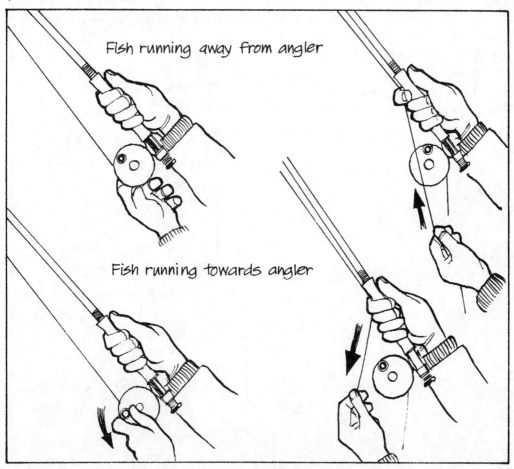

Fish running away from angler

Fish running towards angler

A fish heading for snags can be turned by applying side strain.

Playing and landing

Never attempt to net a trout before it has tired sufficiently to be controlled under the rod-tip. Adopt as low a profile as possible and avoid all unnecessary movement. Draw the fish over the stationary net. Never jab at the fish in an attempt to scoop it out.

For heavy trout, lift the net from the water using the following procedure.

Accessories

LANDING NET: For river and small stream fishing where the angler is constantly on the move, and often up to his knees in water, a collapsible short-handled net is convenient. When fishing a lake the long-handled version is more practical.

River net

Lake net

WAISTCOAT: This is a valuable piece of clothing which enables small, but important bits of equipment to be carried close to hand.

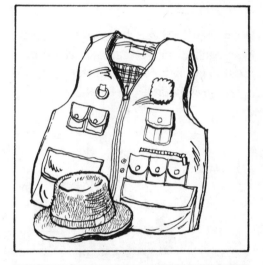

HAT: It is always advisable to wear a hat, especially when fishing a lake where long casts are often necessary; it provides protection as well as shading the eyes.

BINOCULARS: A scan of the water surface with binoculars will often reveal the presence of feeding fish. They are also very useful for insect spotting.

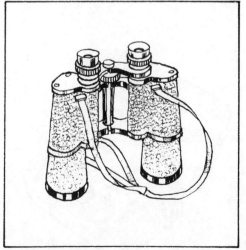

Accessories

SCISSORS: A good quality, sharp pair of scissors are essential for trimming knot ends or clipping unwanted hackle from flies. For safety's sake, stick the points into a cork.

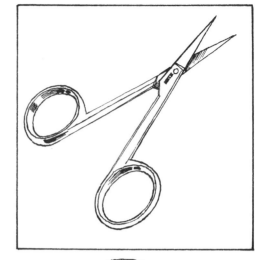

BASS BAG: These bags are sold at many stillwater fisheries, and are the ideal container for retaining your catch and keeping it fresh.

FLY WALLET

FLY BOX

STILLWATER
FLY BOX

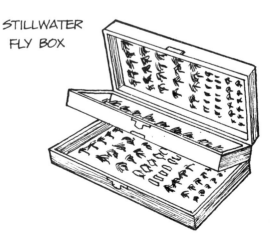

Accessories

LINE TRAY: The ideal receptacle for storing loose line during the retrieve. The alternative is to let the line fall to the ground, where it may become snagged in bank-side undergrowth. Most anglers, however, prefer to fish without a line tray.

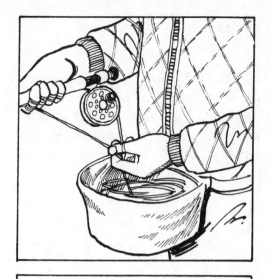

PRIEST: The most humane way of dispatching a trout is to deal it one or two blows on the head with this impliment. Some priests are equipped with a marrow scoop. By inserting the scoop through the mouth and into the stomach of the dead trout a sample of the stomach contents can be withdrawn. A survey will quickly reveal on what insects the trout has been feeding.

Stag Horn Priest

Marrow Scoop / Priest

POLAROID GLASSES: These are invaluable for cutting out glare from the water surface. For stalking clear-water trout they are perfect, as they enable the angler to see into the water.

Knots

BLOOD KNOT: For joining lengths of different breaking strain nylon in order to produce a tapered leader. Recommended breaking strains are shown in another section of this book.

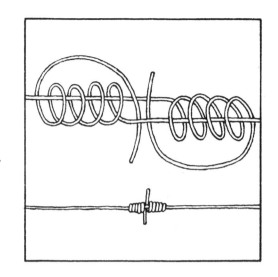

TUCKED HALF-BLOOD KNOT: Unlike the basic half-blood knot, this knot will not slip, and is the ideal knot for connecting a fly to the point or dropper of a leader.

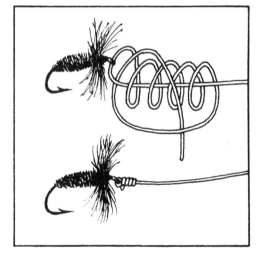

DROPPER KNOT: There is more than one knot can be used for this purpose. The water knot shown, however, permits the use of nylon equal in breaking strain to that of the point to be connected further up, where the main leader is thicker.

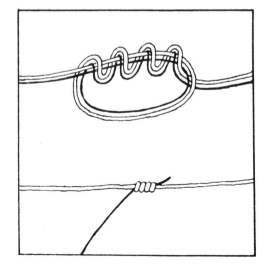

Knots

Here are three more knots which can be used to secure a Fly to a leader. These knots are more suited to small dry Flies — use the tucked half blood knot for larger hooks.

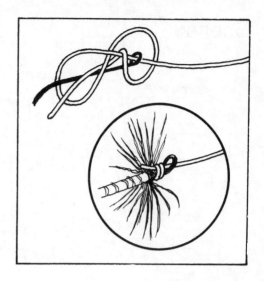

WOOD KNOT

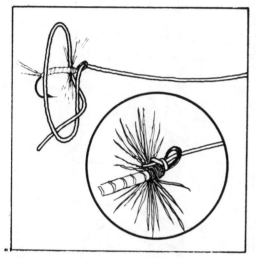

HALF HITCH

TURLE KNOT

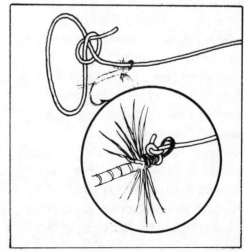

Licence

SOUTH WEST WATER AUTHORITY   **ROD LICENCE**   4704

Licensee's Full Name *(Mr Mr Miss)* ... *Mr. R. HOWARD*

Permanent Address *(Block Letters)* ... *CLEAVE COTTAGE OAKFORD*

Date of Issue *3/5/84*   Time of issue *11-15*

Distributor ... *LINESPORTS*

1984   TROUT ANNUAL   £5·00

How to identify a salmon parr.

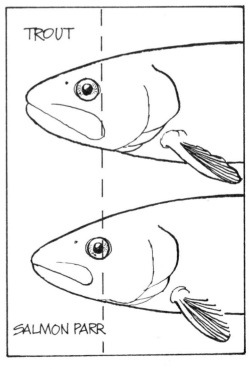

TROUT

SALMON PARR

It is most important that, before you go rushing off to the nearest river to catch a trout, you are in possession of a trout rod licence. Permission is also needed from the riparian owner of the land through which the river flows. If an angling club controls the fishing rights, a permit issued by that club will be required.

Many private and water authority stillwater fisheries issue block permits which include, in the fee, the charge for a rod licence.

A trout licence entitles the licensee to fish for coarse fish and trout, but not salmon or sea trout. Salmon parr accidently caught while trout fishing should be returned to the water.

Water authorities

Ten water authority areas exist in England and Wales, with each area issuing its own licence.

The itinerant angler should therefore ensure that the relevant licence is acquired, before any fishing is done.

NORTH-UMBRIAN

NORTH WEST

YORKSHIRE

SEVERN TRENT

ANGLIAN

WELSH

THAMES

WESSEX

SOUTHERN

SOUTH WEST

SEA
FISHING

Introduction

The sport of angling becomes more popular as leisure time increases, and there is little doubt that sea angling, with its multitude of attendant skills and abilities, is the fastest-growing section of this great sport.

Reasons for this fast-growing popularity are not difficult to find. It is a sport which gets people into the great outdoors, whether it be at sea in a boat, or on a beach or pier. It is also a sport which will stick with you through good times and bad. It can easily be made into a very expensive sport by the acquisition of a fabulous sea-going vessel equipped with the very latest in navigational, communication and fish-finding equipment; or it can be made to fit the slimmest of budgets by making the most of your own gear, digging your own bait and fishing from rocks, beaches or piers close to home.

Broadly speaking, sea angling can be divided into two categories, boat fishing and shore fishing, and they are two distinctly different branches of the sport.

The boat angler either owns a boat, or pays his share of a charter fee and fishes from a charter boat. These are usually run by a professional skipper whose livelihood depends on putting his clients over a spot which is known to hold fish. Charter boats vary considerably in size. There are small, inshore boats which rarely venture more than 10 or 12 miles from their home port. And at the other end of the scale there are boats equipped with a Decca navigational system, professional echo sounders, and so on.

These go 50 miles or more offshore to fish deepwater wrecks, often in water over 40 fathoms deep, in search of supersize pollack, cod, coalfish, or perhaps that ferocious denizen of the deep, the conger eel.

Boat anglers who own their boats are a breed apart. Not only do they have to know how to catch fish, but they must also be accomplished seamen, navigators, amateur shipwrights and mechanics – skills all too easily overlooked by the layman as he casually observes the angler unloading his catch.

Shore anglers also need to acquire skills not readily appreciated by the casual observer. These range from the delicate craft required to catch the grey ghost of inshore waters, the mullet, to the considerable athletic ability required to propel 5 oz (150 g) of lead some 100 yd or more, out behind the foaming surf.

There is another side to shore angling: often the best fish come from little-frequented beaches or headlands which sometimes require a hike of several miles, often over some rough terrain, so a good degree of physical fitness is required. And if you don't believe that, just try carrying a 30 or 40 lb (13.5 or 18 kg) pack half a mile along a shingle beach!

Newcomers to the sport often naively believe that if they buy the latest carbon fibre rod, a super reel, and all that goes with them, they are guaranteed to catch fish. Then they find that the veteran angler with his tatty old tackle can outfish them hands down. At this point the newcomer will either give up in disgust, or take his first step in learning what this great sport is all about, by confessing his ignorance to the veteran and asking his advice. Most times he will receive more help than he can assimilate, as well as an earbashing about how good it was in years gone by, but that is all part of the fishing scene.

From that moment, the fishing bug will begin to bite deep into your conscious life. You will discover that being an angler is more 'a way of life' than just a hobby, as it is so casually described by those who know no better. Your whole life will start to be governed by the state of the tide, wind and weather, to an extent beyond the comprehension of even your nearest and dearest. Those moments of minor triumph over the weekend will be with you through the week, giving rise to rumours among your workmates that you are a 'fishing nut'; but if you are one, you won't worry much about that.

It is recognized that in all sports, there is a hard core of knowledge, skills and physical abilities which must be learnt or developed in order to progress to genuine mastery and full realization of one's potential.

There are two levels of fishing knowledge: the overt kind, which can be learnt from books and evening classes; and the covert kind, which cannot be readily seen, and which can only be learnt through detailed observation and actual experience.

At some time or other we have all heard the tale of one angler catching fish, and another standing alongside him, using identical tackle and bait from the same bait box, who cannot catch a fish however hard he tries. This is a typical example of a covert skill. The first angler probably doesn't realize exactly what he is doing, he just knows that, whatever it is, it works.

Experience is the best teacher of any practical skill, and this is especially true of outdoor sports, particularly angling. You have to be out there in wind and weather, handling the boat, watching the compass and echo sounder, or prowling the beach or cliff top watching for nature's signs that the fish are feeding. A cloud of gulls wheeling and diving over the great green Atlantic rollers as the bass play in and out of them, cutting up the shoals of sandeels and britt; these scavengers give the game away by feeding on the debris as it floats to the surface. A crack-of-dawn stroll along the beach after a storm at sea will reveal the washed-up debris before the sea-shore scavengers destroy the evidence of what the fish are feeding on, out there behind the third breaker: perhaps a hermit crab, razorfish, scallop or crab. All are nature's clues, and should be acted upon, not next week, not tomorrow, but right at that instant. The fish will be there, looking for more tasty morsels.

This book doesn't hide what it says behind a hedge of words. Each picture is a statement which makes for clear and easy understanding, and forms a good base on which to build your practical experience.

Nice one Tony,

Russ Symons,
Plymouth, Devon

Rods

BEACHCASTER:
This rod is designed to throw a bait a long way. Distance is all important if the fish are feeding 100yd (27.8m) plus from the shoreline.
Lengths vary from 11ft (3.50m) to 15ft (4.55m).

BOAT ROD:
Boat rods are shorter than beachcasters, 7ft 6in (2.30m) being about the average length. Some are equipped with rings throughout, some have rings with a roller at the tip, and others have rollers from tip to butt.

SPINNING ROD:
This is a useful addition to any sea-angler's armoury, for casting a spinner or float tackle. There are many good hollow-glass spinning rods to choose from; solid glass rods should be avoided.

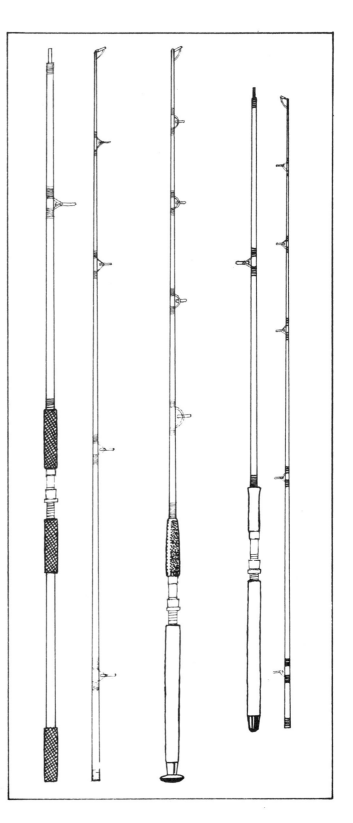

Reels

FIXED SPOOL: This is the ideal reel for the beginner, providing trouble-free casting, and capable of casting a bait considerable distances. For maximum efficiency the reel should be loaded correctly; the procedure for doing this is shown on a later page.

BEACH MULTIPLIER: In the hands of an expert, this reel is second to none, both in distance-casting ability, and for providing direct and positive contact with the bait and fish. Here again, the reel's performance is affected if the spool is not correctly loaded.

BOAT MULTIPLIER: Unlike the beach multiplier, this type of reel is not designed for casting but for presenting a lure or bait beneath a boat. There are variations of this reel, some more suited to bottom fishing, and others to trolling. They also come in different sizes, from the smaller, light-line capacity to the large, big-game models. Manufacturers' catalogues supply detailed specifications.

How to load a reel

FIXED SPOOL

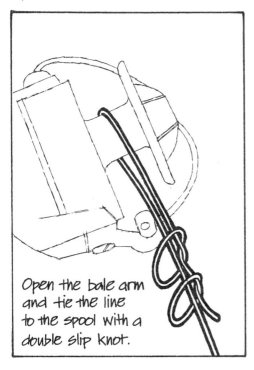

Open the bale arm and tie the line to the spool with a double slip knot.

MULTIPLIER

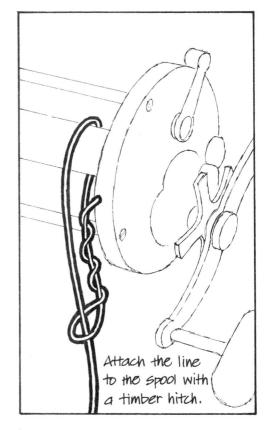

Attach the line to the spool with a timber hitch.

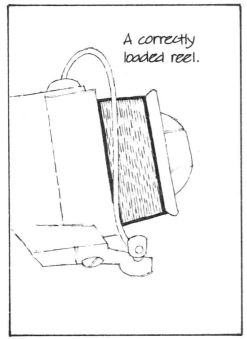

A correctly loaded reel.

Load to within ¼in (3mm) below the spool rim.

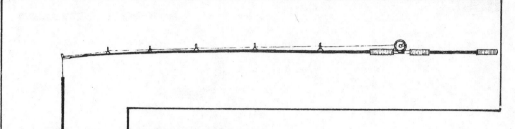

Shock leader

This consists of 30ft (9.15m) of stronger line connected to the main line. Its function is to absorb the shock and stress of casting with a beachcaster. The breaking strain of the shock leader will depend on the weight of the lead. As a yardstick, if a weight of 6oz (180g) is being used, the breaking strain of the shock leader needs to be about 50lb (23kg). The shock leader should be attached to the main line correctly to ensure the knot does not foul on the rod rings during the cast.

Leader   Main line

To avoid injury to the thumb during the cast the knot should be tucked to one side of the reel spool.

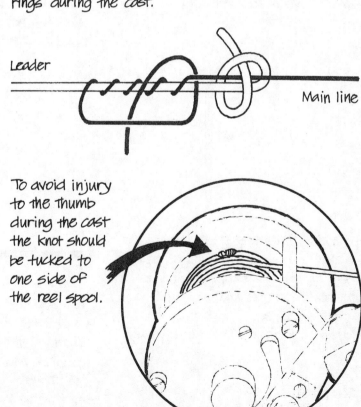

Hooks

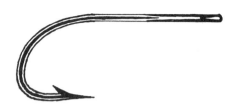

O'SHAUGHNESSY: An ideal hook for boat legering when fishing for conger and ling over rocky ground.

FINE WIRE ABERDEEN: This is the ideal hook for most light shore-fishing where the seabed is clean. It is the best hook for threading on a lugworm or ragworm bait, and is also ideal for livebaiting with a sandeel when boat fishing.

BAIT-HOLDER: This hook is very widely used, but the cuts in the shank probably do more harm than good by creating weak points.

FORGED STAINLESS STEEL: Where the seabed is rougher, or where large bass or cod are expected, this is the best hook for the job. In its larger sizes, eg., 7/0 or 8/0, it is capable of dealing with shore conger.

SEAMASTER: The 'big daddy' of sea hooks. It is used in conjunction with a cable-laid wire trace, and is the only reliable hook to use for wreck conger, or shark. This hook ranges in size from 4/0 to a massive 16/0.

Hook sizes and anatomy

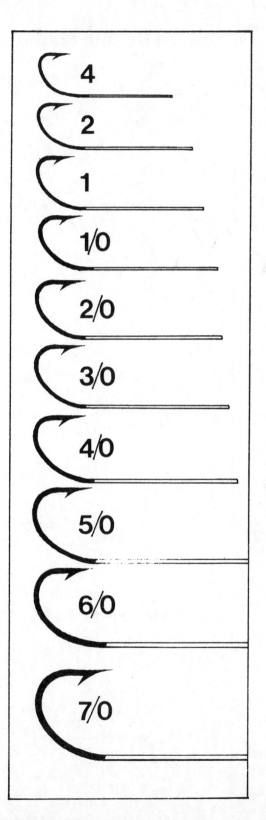

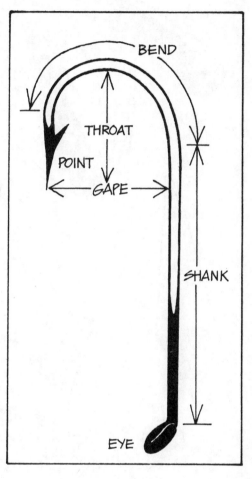

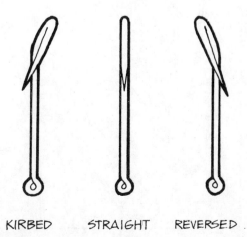

KIRBED   STRAIGHT   REVERSED

Shore fishing leads

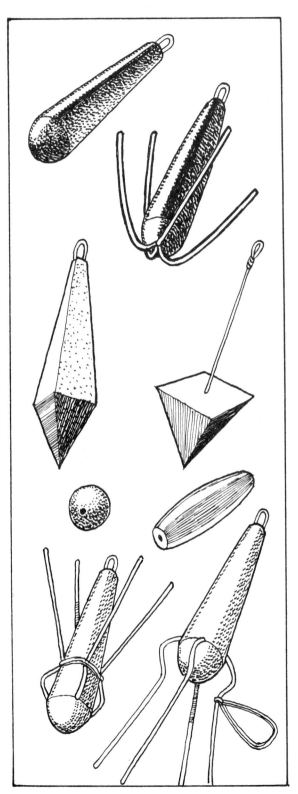

Casting bomb

Bomb with grip wires

Torpedo

Pyramid standfast

Drilled bullet

Barrel

'Breakaway' casting bomb

Closed   Open

Boat fishing leads

Some of the weights shown under the heading of shore-fishing can also be used for presenting a bait from a boat.

The drilled bullet, for example, is the best lead for keeping a live sandeel at the required depth.

Casting bombs can also be used in conjunction with a paternoster rig.

When trolling for bass over and around reefs, the spiral weight (shown opposite) is the number one choice.

Where a positive hold on the bottom is required, when legering in deep water with a strong tidal flow, the pyramid or grip lead should be used.

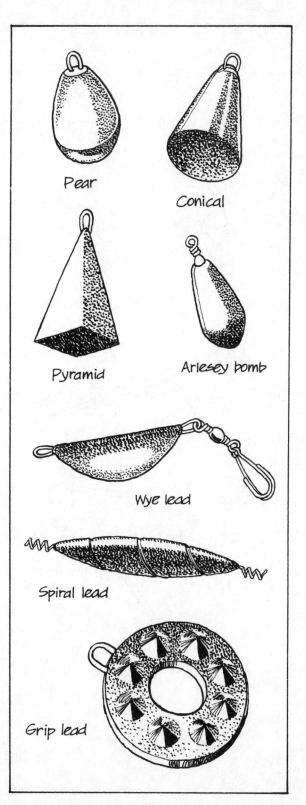

Pear

Conical

Pyramid

Arlesey bomb

Wye lead

Spiral lead

Grip lead

Links and swivels

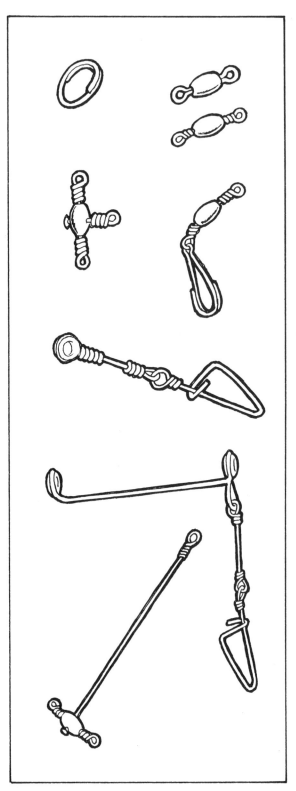

Split link

Barrel swivels

Three-way swivel

Link swivel

Kilmore link

Clement's boom

Three-way swivel boom

Shore terminal tackle

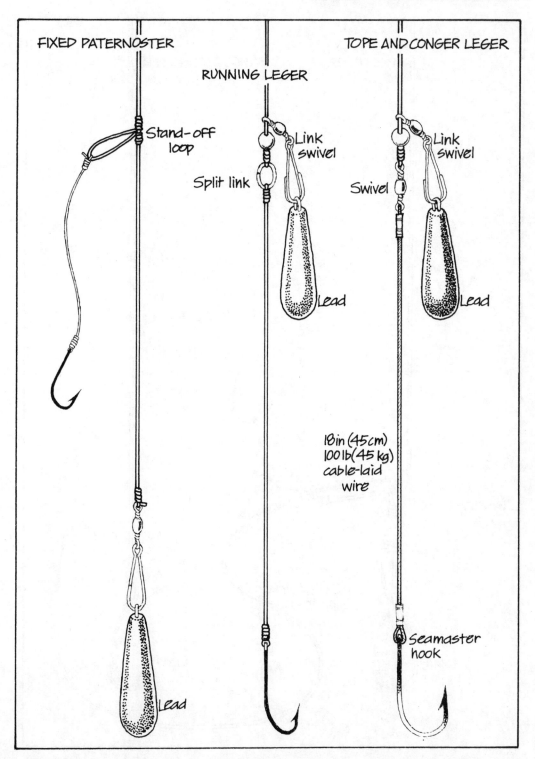

FIXED PATERNOSTER

Stand-off loop

Lead

Lead

RUNNING LEGER

Link swivel

Split link

Lead

TOPE AND CONGER LEGER

Link swivel

Swivel

Lead

18in (45cm)
100lb (45kg)
cable-laid
wire

Seamaster hook

Boat terminal tackle

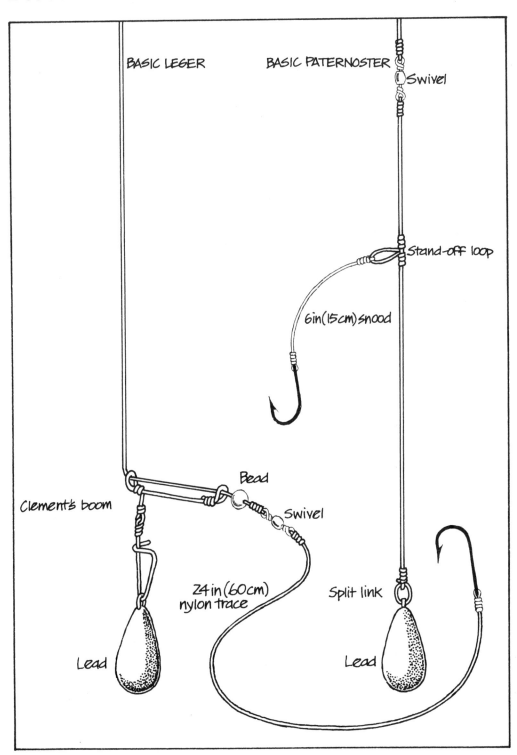

BASIC LEGER

BASIC PATERNOSTER

Swivel

Stand-off loop

6in (15cm) snood

Bead

Clement's boom

Swivel

24in (60cm)
nylon trace

Split link

Lead

Lead

Boat terminal tackle

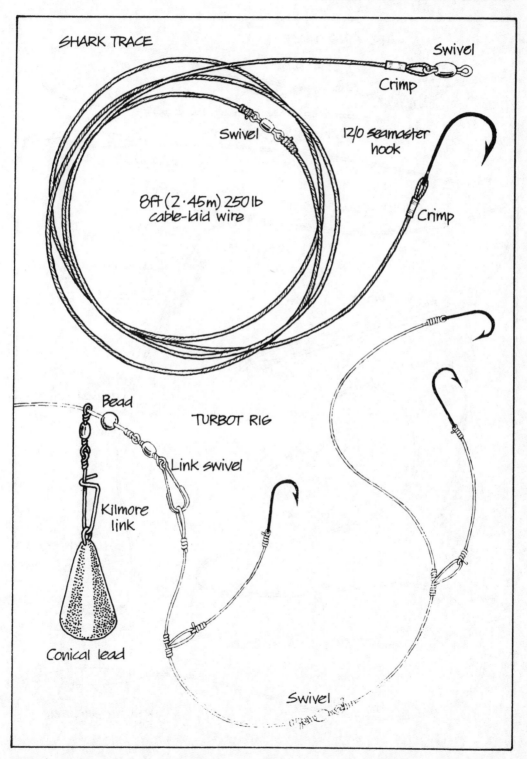

SHARK TRACE

Swivel

Crimp

Swivel

12/0 seamaster hook

Crimp

8ft (2·45m) 250lb cable-laid wire

Bead

TURBOT RIG

Link swivel

Kilmore link

Conical lead

Swivel

Boat terminal tackle

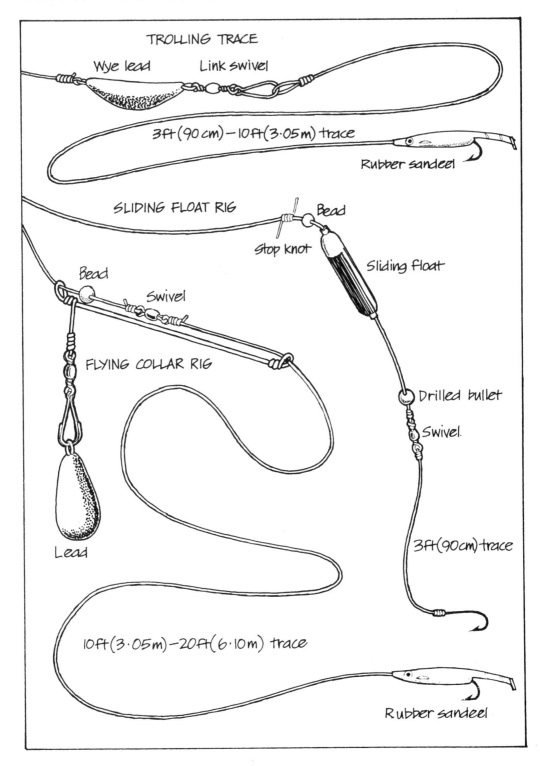

TROLLING TRACE

Wye lead Link swivel

3ft (90 cm) – 10ft (3.05 m) trace

Rubber sandeel

SLIDING FLOAT RIG Bead

Stop knot

Sliding float

Bead

Swivel

FLYING COLLAR RIG

Drilled bullet

Swivel.

Lead

3ft (90cm) trace

10ft (3.05m) – 20ft (6.10m) trace

Rubber sandeel

Species

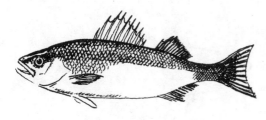

BASS Are found in greatest numbers in Atlantic coastal waters. They love to cruise around reefs, and often enter estuaries, where they follow the tide for many miles upstream.

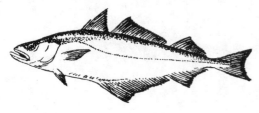

POLLACK A fish of rocks, reefs and wrecks. They are common all around the British Isles and the coast of Europe. Smaller pollack can even be found over a clean sandy bottom.

COALFISH Very similar to the pollack. The coalfish, however, has a straight, light-coloured lateral line, whilst the pollack has a dark lateral line with a kink near the shoulder.

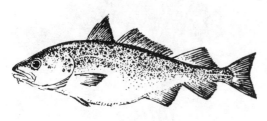

COD A fish that is widely distributed around Britain and Northern Europe. Offshore boat anglers can contact them all year round, but the shore angler has to wait for the colder months.

WHITING This greedy fish can be found just about anywhere during the winter months. It will grab both worm and fish bait, especially after dark.

POUTING Sometimes known as pout or bib, this ravenous little fish is probably more of a pest than any other fish that swims in the sea. Unfortunately it is very prolific.

Species

HADDOCK Not so widely distributed as the whiting, but common north of Biscay, where it is of great commercial value.

MACKEREL During the summer mackerel shoals harry small fry around the coasts of Britain and Europe. They will often drive the fry on to beaches, and will follow them well upstream in an estuary.

GREY MULLET A fish of estuaries, lagoons, harbours and backwaters. They are also found all around the coastline, where they browse on weed.

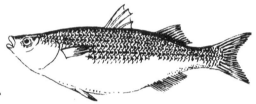

BALLAN WRASSE This handsome fish is found only among rocks, and in water of a reasonable depth. It is mainly an Atlantic fish, but the North Sea has a few off the East coast of Scotland.

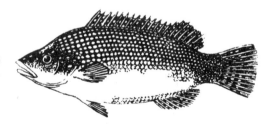

BLACK BREAM A warm-water, summer visitor to northern European waters. It likes to shoal up around wrecks and rocky outcrops.

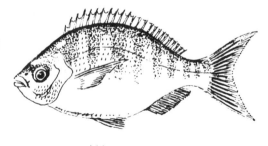

RED BREAM Another summer visitor to northern European waters, but not as common as the black bream.

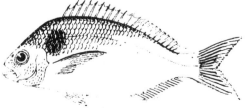

Species

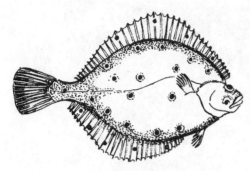

PLAICE Instantly recognizable by the large orange or red spots on the back. They will move in over sandbanks and mudbanks on a rising tide, where they feed on cockles, worms and crustaceans.

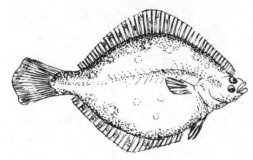

FLOUNDER This is a drab fish compared to the plaice. Some do have reddish spots, but these fade after the fish has been out of the water for some time.

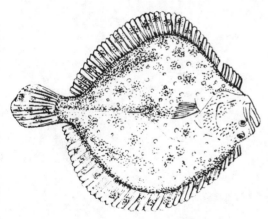

TURBOT This big predator lives on gravel, shell and sandy bottoms. It feeds heavily on other small fish, such as sandeels, sprats, herring, whiting and pout.

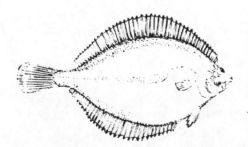

DAB A small flatfish, but what it lacks in size it makes up for in taste (the flesh is delicious). They prefer shallow water with a sandy bottom, and will provide non-stop sport for the angler who is lucky to fish such a place when the dabs are hungry.

Species

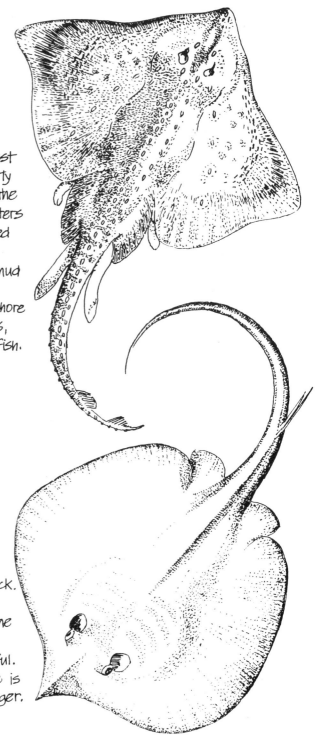

THORNBACK RAY The commonest of all the rays. They are instantly recognizable by the spines along the back. They move into inshore waters with the arrival of spring and feed mainly over clear, sandy areas. Occasionally they will live over mud or gravel, but shun rocky areas completely. Their diet includes shore crabs, shrimps, sandeels, herrings, sprats, and various other small fish. It also goes under the name of 'roker' in some areas.

STINGRAY A later visitor to inshore waters than the thornback. Food consists mainly of molluscs and crustaceans. The spine on the tail is venomous and any injury inflicted by it is extremely painful. Sometimes more than one spine is present, thus increasing the danger.

Species

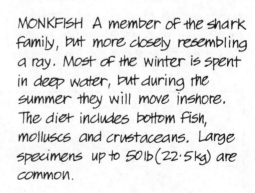

SKATE This is the largest member of the ray family. They live in deeper water than the thornback and stingray. A specimen of 100lb (45 kg) is not uncommon. They feed mainly on bottom-living fish, crabs and various worms.

MONKFISH A member of the shark family, but more closely resembling a ray. Most of the winter is spent in deep water, but during the summer they will move inshore. The diet includes bottom fish, molluscs and crustaceans. Large specimens up to 50lb (22·5 kg) are common.

Species

SPUR-DOG

A very common member of the shark family, with a venomous spine on each dorsal fin. They form large packs and hunt over a soft bottom, consuming sprats, sandeels, herring, garfish, bottom fish and crabs. The average weight is 14lb (6·3 kg).

LESSER-SPOTTED DOGFISH

Very common around the coast of Britain and Europe. They hunt over sand, gravel or mud, and feed on crabs, shrimps, molluscs and worms. The greater spotted dogfish, known also as nursehound, or bull huss, is less common than the lesser spotted variety, but, as the name implies, grows to a larger size.

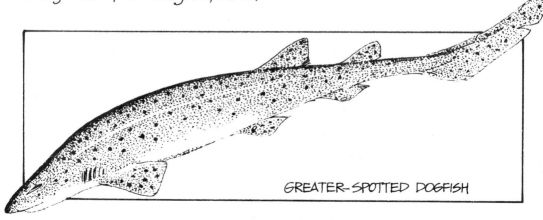

GREATER-SPOTTED DOGFISH

Species

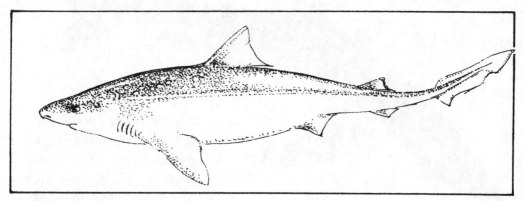

SMOOTH HOUND

Two species of smooth hound are to be found in British and European waters: the common smooth hound, (Mustelus mustelus), and the starry smooth hound, (M. asterias). They live in comparatively shallow water near the shore-line where they feed on hermit crabs, other small crabs and lobsters. Bottom-feeding fish also form part of their diet.

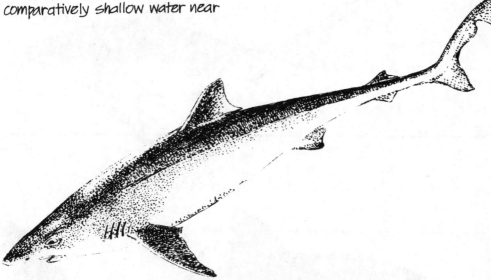

TOPE

Shallow water is favoured by this small shark. It forms small packs and hunts small fish such as whiting and pouting. Bottom-living fish also form part of the diet, along with crustaceans. They are a sizeable fish, 50lb (23kg) or 60lb (27kg) not being uncommon.

Species

BLUE SHARK

These sharks are all summer visitors to Northern European waters, where they hunt shoals of mackerel and herring. They all live in the open sea and migrate many miles every year.

THRESHER SHARK

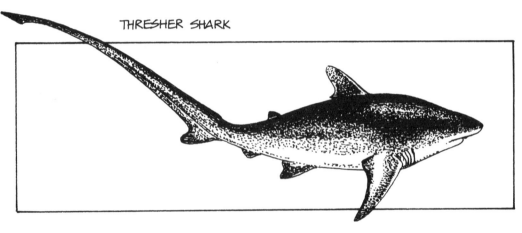

PORBEAGLE SHARK

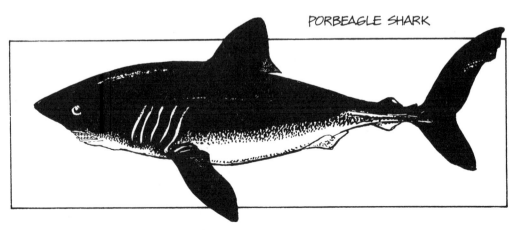

CONGER AND LING

Species

These two heavyweights live among the wrecks of ships, which are scattered over the seabed from the Bay of Biscay to the North Sea. The tangled hulks of sunken merchant and naval craft provide a haven for small fish, and this in turn presents easy pickings for these predators.

Bait

Crab

Peeler and softback crabs are the finest bait for most species of shore-caught fish. A crab is a peeler when it is in the process of losing its old shell. To test if a crab is a peeler, try lifting the rear end of the shell; it should come away easily.

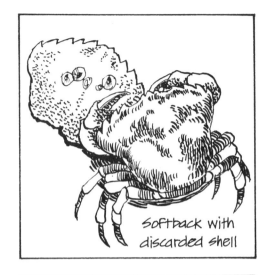

Softback with discarded shell

When a crab has discarded its old shell it is known as a softback. During this stage it is very vulnerable to attack, and can often be found hiding beneath a larger hardback. Both peelers and softbacks can be found beneath the weed on rocky foreshores. They will also bury themselves in mud.

To keep crabs alive and fresh, put them in a bucket or box, introduce some damp sea-weed and cover the container with an old towel which has been saturated in sea water. Store in a cool, dark place.

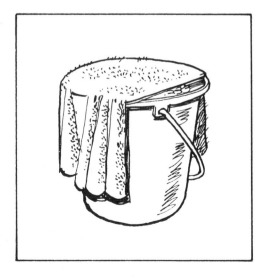

Bait

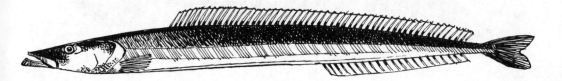

Sandeel

This excellent bait can be collected from wet sand, where it lies buried on a receding tide, or purchased from the local seine-netters. They can be used as a dead bait, but are far more effective live.

To keep them alive, store them in a special bait bucket which has a battery-operated aerator to keep the water well oxygenated.

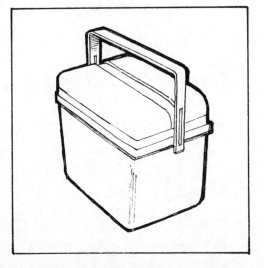

They will also survive in an ice box. Any surplus eels can be put into a freezer and used as deadbait at a later date.

Bait

Lugworm

The lugworm lives in a 'U'-shaped burrow beneath the sand or mud. The colonies are exposed at low tide, and are evident by the casts.

Blow hole   Cast

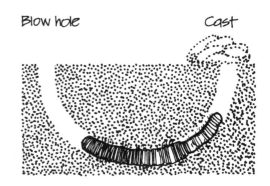

They can be kept fresh for a few days in sheets of newspaper, or for a longer period in fresh sea-water plus an aerator pump.

Dig with a broad-tined fork or a spade around the blow hole and the cast.

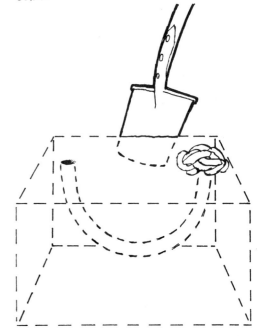

202

Bait

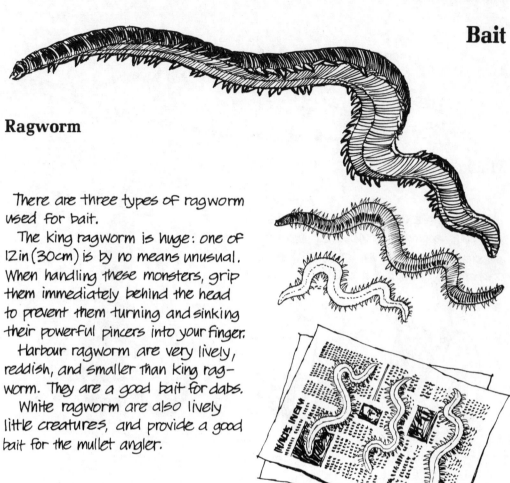

Ragworm

There are three types of ragworm used for bait.

The king ragworm is huge: one of 12in (30cm) is by no means unusual. When handling these monsters, grip them immediately behind the head to prevent them turning and sinking their powerful pincers into your finger.

Harbour ragworm are very lively, reddish, and smaller than king rag-worm. They are a good bait for dabs.

White ragworm are also lively little creatures, and provide a good bait for the mullet angler.

King ragworm live in a mixture of mud and shale. No small amount of physical exertion is required to ex-tricate them with a fork. On occas-ions though, they can be exposed by simply lifting a rock.

The other two types of ragworm can be found on estuary mud-flats at low tide, by digging with a fork or spade.

Ragworms are hardier than lugs and can be kept for a longer period. Check daily though, and discard any that are dead or mutilated.

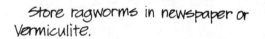

Store ragworms in newspaper or Vermiculite.

Bait

Mackerel

This is an excellent bait for many sea fish, especially the deep-water species. There are various ways of presenting it on the hook.

Whole side fillet

Chunk

Hook-size fillet

Belly sliver

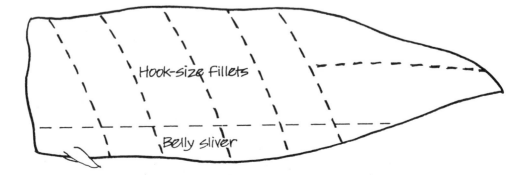

Hook-size fillets

Belly sliver

Squid

Bait

Like mackerel, squid can be mounted on the hook in various ways, to cater for different-sized fish.

Body

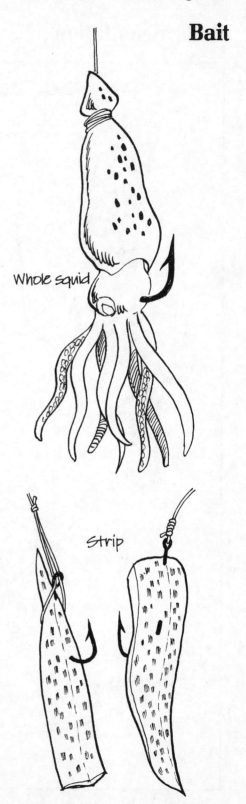

Whole squid

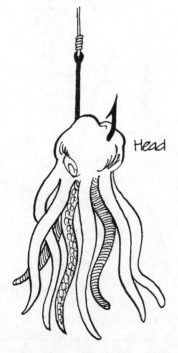

Head

Strip

Bait presentation

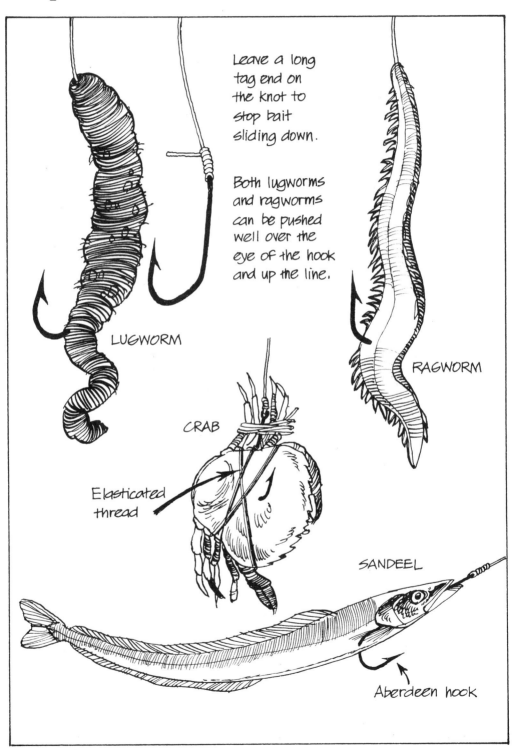

Leave a long tag end on the knot to stop bait sliding down.

Both lugworms and ragworms can be pushed well over the eye of the hook and up the line.

LUGWORM

RAGWORM

CRAB

Elasticated thread

SANDEEL

Aberdeen hook

Bait clips

The clip is held in position by a short length of rubber tubing. Bait clips prevent tangles and cut down drag as the tackle flies through the air during a cast. This allows longer casts to be made. When the tackle hits the water, the hooks come free and the snoods resume their normal position.

A sliding stop knot above the hook prevents the bait from sliding too far up the line.

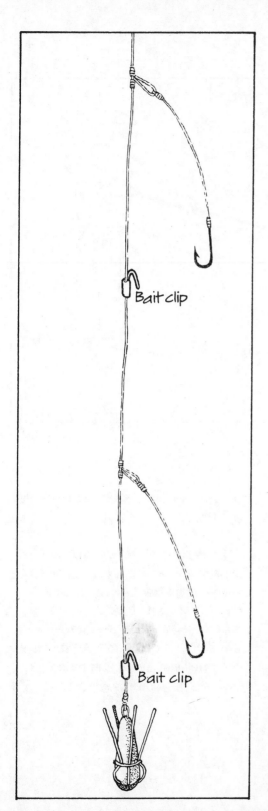

Bait clip

Bait clip

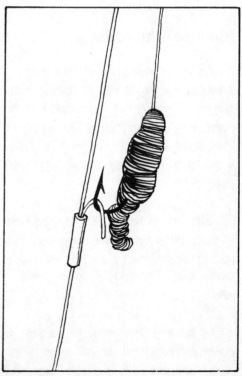

Casting

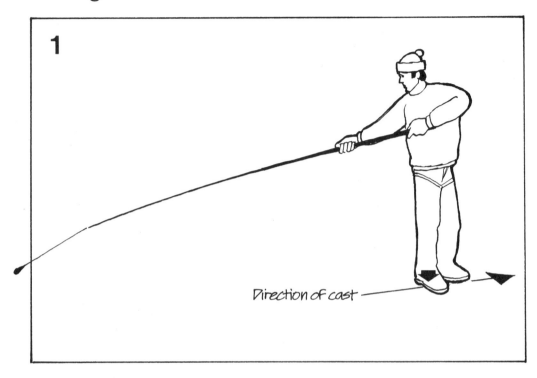

1

Direction of cast

Basic off-the-ground cast

① Adopt a position with the left shoulder facing in the direction of the target. Turn to the right, and with the right arm fully extended, swing the lead back so that it is lying on the ground. Your weight should be on the right foot.

② Turn the head to look towards the target. Firmly, and smoothly, pull the rod up and forward, and at the same time swivel the body around to the left.

③ As the left arm straightens pull it down strongly and at the same time push forward with the right arm. All the body-weight should now be on the left foot.

The basic off-the-ground cast is capable of producing casts of 100yd (91·5m) and more. Dirty, rough, steeply-shelving beaches, however, tend to reduce the efficiency of this cast. To overcome this problem the pendulum swing can be added, and this is shown overleaf.

Casting

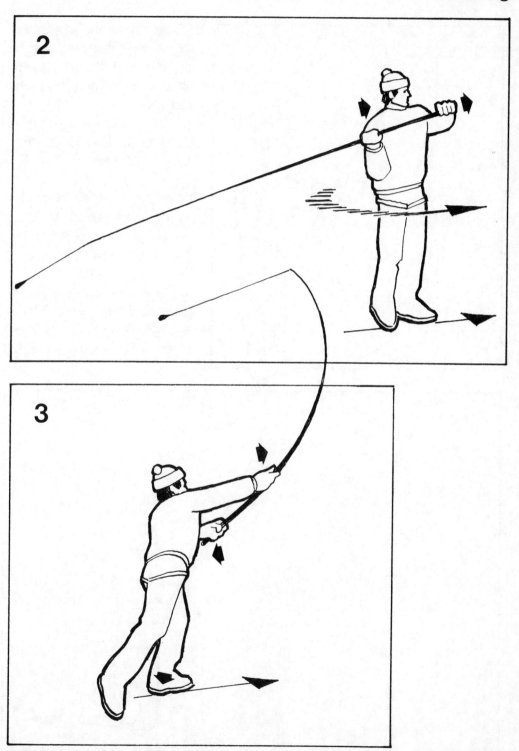

Pendulum cast

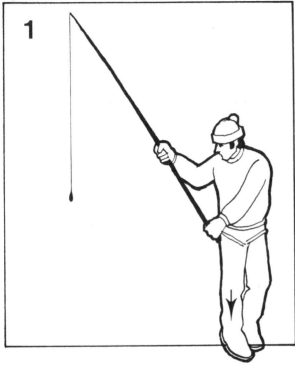

① Adopt the same position as for the off-the-ground cast, but this time hold the rod up, with about 6ft (1·85m) between tip and lead.

② Swing the lead to the left, then to the right.

③ At the top of the right hand swing, lower the rod to the second position of the off-the-ground cast.

④ The transition from one phase to another should be done smoothly to finish in the power-drive towards the target.

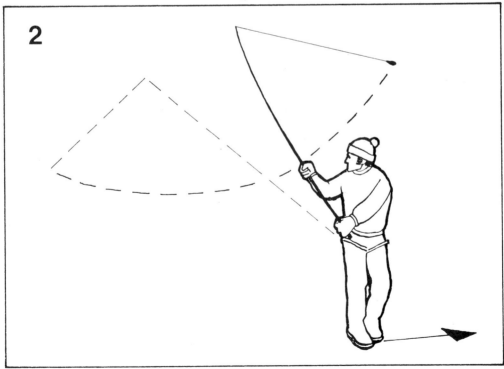

Casting

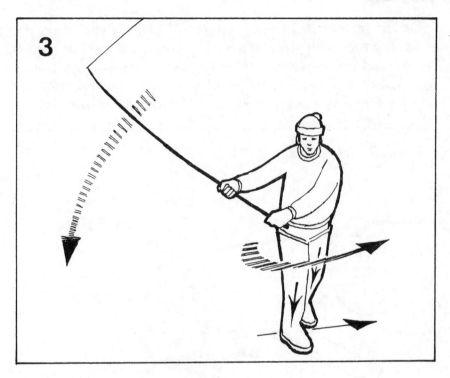

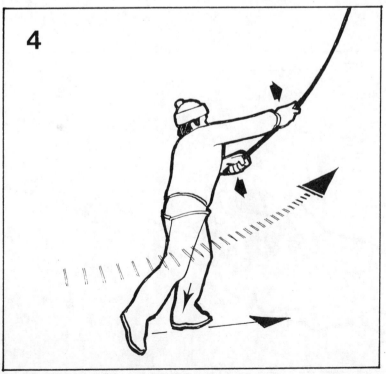

Casting

The line release and follow-through is the same for both types of cast. As the lead passes the rod-tip, release line from the forefinger if using a fixed-spool, or the thumb if using a multiplier. Trap the line again as the lead hits the water. When the lead has sunk to the sea-bed, take up the slack line with a few turns of the reel handle.

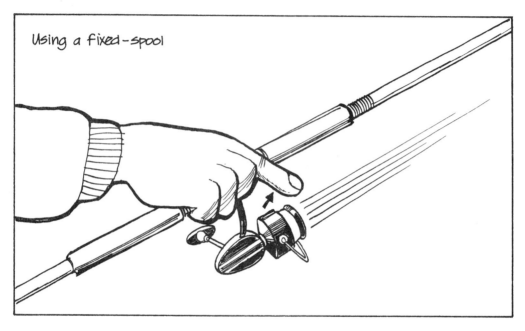

Using a fixed-spool

Using a multiplier

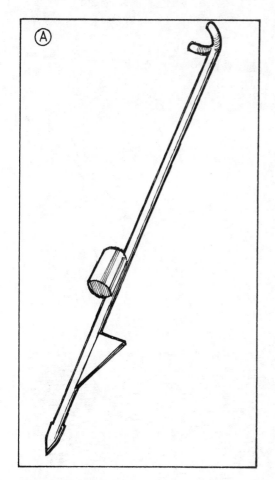

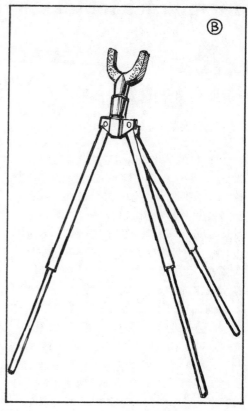

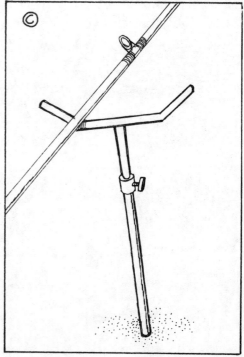

Rod rests

Ⓐ The monopod is ideal in firm sand and mud, but is not suited to hard surfaces and very large pebbles.

Ⓑ The tripod, however, will cope with most surfaces and is probably the most sensible choice for the newcomer.

Ⓒ This very basic but useful rest is popular with many top beach anglers. It allows the rod to be propped at a variety of angles.

Yarmouth back-cast

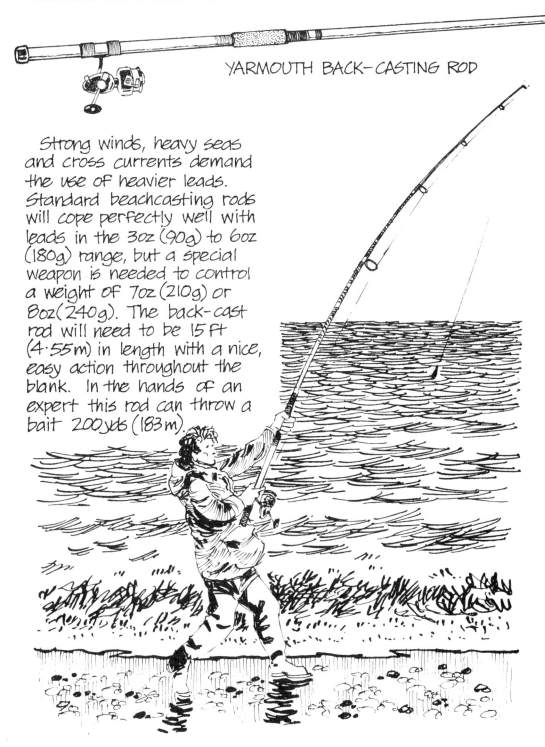

YARMOUTH BACK-CASTING ROD

Strong winds, heavy seas and cross currents demand the use of heavier leads. Standard beachcasting rods will cope perfectly well with leads in the 3oz (90g) to 6oz (180g) range, but a special weapon is needed to control a weight of 7oz (210g) or 8oz (240g). The back-cast rod will need to be 15ft (4.55m) in length with a nice, easy action throughout the blank. In the hands of an expert this rod can throw a bait 200 yds (183m).

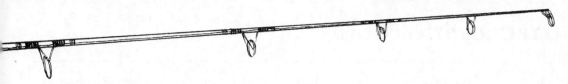

Most long-distance casters cut the bale arm from a fixed-spool reel before any casting is done. This eliminates the risk of the bale arm snapping over half-way through a cast, invariably resulting in a lost lead, shock leader and terminal tackle.

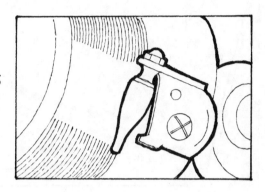

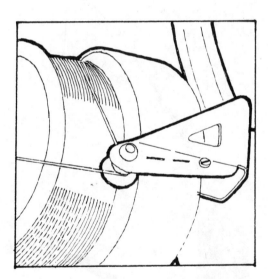

The Mitchell 498 fixed-spool beach reel has a specially-designed manual pick-up device as an integral feature.

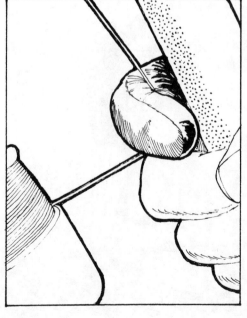

To avoid injury during the cast, the index finger should be protected with a finger stall. The clutch on the spool should also be tightened to maximum setting prior to making the cast.

Yarmouth back-cast

2 Lower the rod and push the weight forward.

1 Stand in a relaxed position and hold the rod almost upright.

3 Throw the lead away to the right and lower the rod.

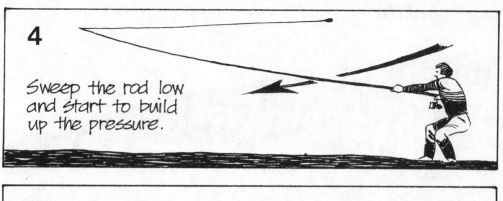

4

Sweep the rod low and start to build up the pressure.

5

Start to lift the rod and continue to build up pressure.

6

Continue to build up pressure until the release — start to turn the body at this point.

7

Point the rod in the direction of the released lead.

Cast control

Even if the bale arm on a fixed-spool reel has been cut away, the pick-up should still be clicked into the open position during the cast. The forefinger is gripping the line and the spool clutch is tightened to maximum setting.

At the point of release the forefinger is straightened, allowing line to flow freely from the spool. Timing the point of release to produce long-distance casts can only come by trial and error.

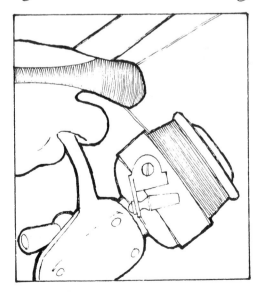

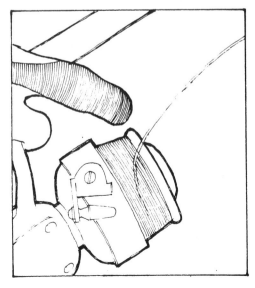

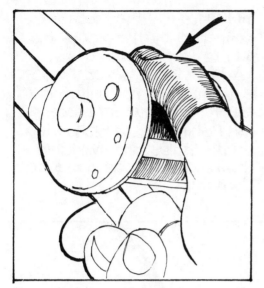

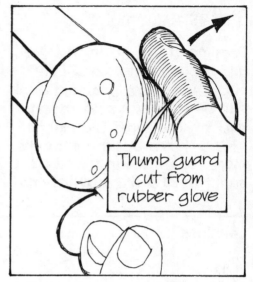

Thumb guard
cut from
rubber glove

When casting with a multiplier, the thumb should be firmly clamped down on the reel line, until the moment of release. The ratchet must be in the off position.

The line is released by lifting the thumb. Light thumb pressure may be necessary, as the lead nears the end of its aerial arc, in order to prevent an overrun.

Trouble-free casts with a multiplier can only be achieved by trial and error and tuning the reel. Most good multipliers incorporate centrifugal brakes which dampen the speed of the rotating spool during a surge. Practise in an open field or along a deserted beach will hopefully iron out any faults, and prepare the angler to fish with confidence.

Tuning a magnetic reel is easily done by adjusting the magnet control screw.

MAGNET CONTROL

Tides

Spring tides are high tides, and occur at new and full moon, when the gravitational pull of both sun and moon are in line with the earth.

Neap tides occur when the moon is in its first, or last quarter and the gravitational influence of the moon is tempered by the pull of the sun.

A knowledge of local tides is invaluable, not only for safety sake but for successful fishing and bait collecting.

Tide tables are available from fishing tackle shops or chandlers.

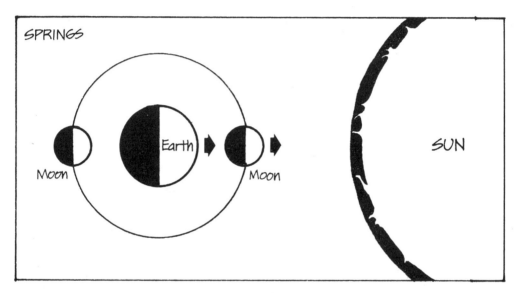

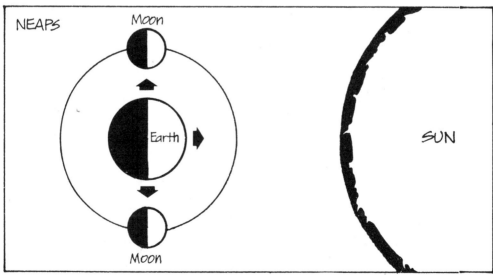

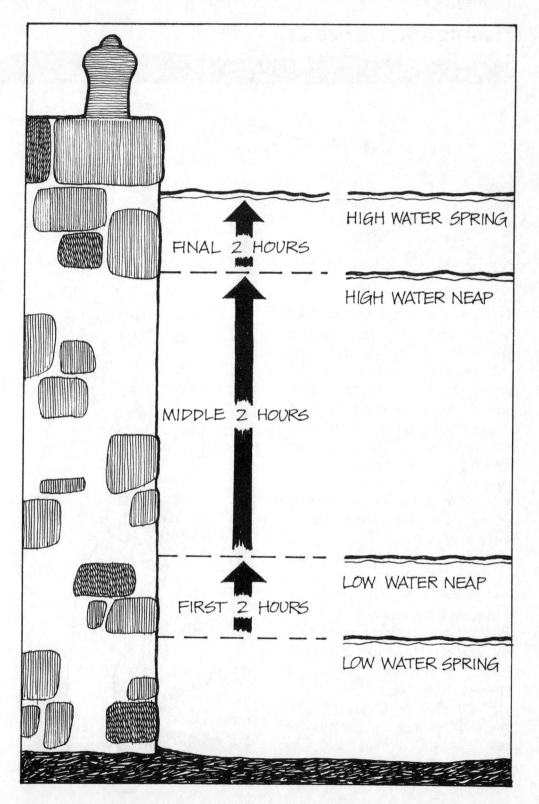

HIGH WATER SPRING

FINAL 2 HOURS

HIGH WATER NEAP

MIDDLE 2 HOURS

LOW WATER NEAP

FIRST 2 HOURS

LOW WATER SPRING

Fishing a storm beach

Storm beaches are exposed to the relentless pounding of the Atlantic Ocean. Long, open expanses of sand expose the angler to the brunt of westerly winds. Rank upon rank of breakers thunder across the strand and die in a table of hissing foam. At times, during settled weather, the roar of the ocean subsides, and wavelets whisper and lap where sand meets water.

However, it is the movement of the surf which dislodges and exposes food over the sandy bottom, therefore it is when the surf is running that the angler will stand a better chance of making contact with fish such as bass.

When fishing from a storm beach it is most important to wear suitable warm and waterproof clothing.

Woolly hat

Polo-neck sweater

Waxed cotton or PVC jacket with hood

Thigh or chest waders

Bass Although other types of fish can be caught from a storm beach, bass are the predominant species. During the summer and autumn these spiny buccaneers move in with the rising tide and hunt for the tasty morsels which are scoured from the sea-bed. Lugworms, crabs, razorfish and sandeels all feature on the menu.

223

Hotspots on a storm beach

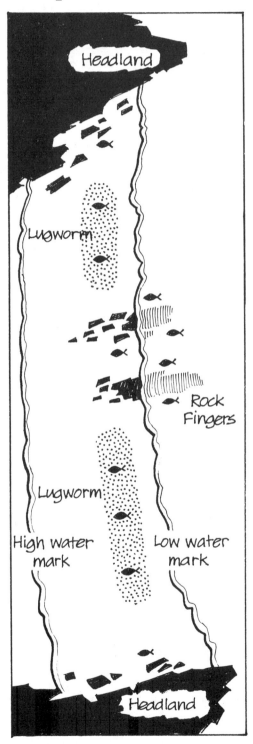

When visiting an unfamiliar beach the angler will benefit by making a reconnaissance at low tide, for this exposed area of beach will become the feeding area for the fish as the tide advances over the sand.

Alongside rock fingers are favourite feeding areas for bass, as crabs are often washed from their hiding places beneath weed or in rock crannies.

This low tide period can also be put to good use by looking for bait such as crab, lugworm, razorfish or sandeel.

Most good storm beach anglers use the multiplier reel which provides a more positive contact when working a fish back through heavy surf. The rod is held whilst waiting for a bite; the fore-finger and thumb feel the line for the pull of a biting bass.

A cast just beyond the third breaker will usually make contact with feeding fish.

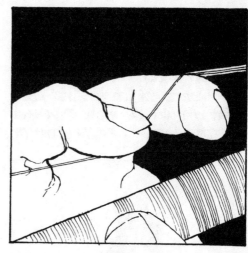

225

Terminal tackle for storm beach bass should be kept as simple as possible.

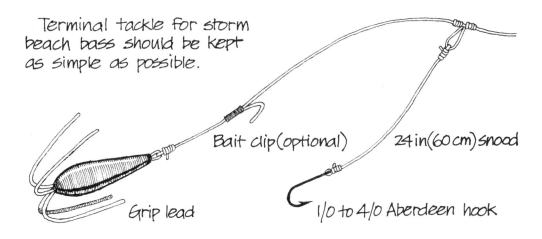

Bait clip (optional)

24 in (60 cm) snood

Grip lead

1/0 to 4/0 Aberdeen hook

A large, juicy lugworm is the ideal bait for storm beach bass, but crab will be just as deadly in areas close to fingers of rock. The hook point should be well exposed to provide positive penetration.

The inclusion of a bait clip on the terminal rig will ensure that the bait stays intact during the surge of the cast. At the end of the cast the hook will fall free of its own accord.

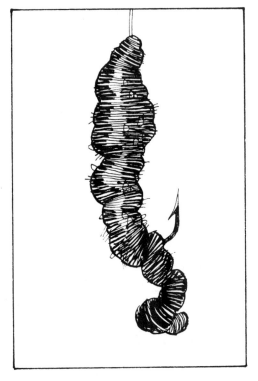

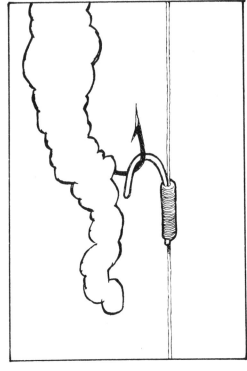

A feeding bass will usually signal his presence with one or two knocks followed by a run. Be prepared for the run and strike the moment it starts. Take a few backward steps at the same time.

When the bass shows signs of tiring, harness the power of the waves to help carry the fish closer to the shore.

Eventually a receding wave will leave the fish high-and-dry and it can be scooped up and carried clear of the water.

Wear a thick leather glove for lifting bass clear of the water to avoid injury from the fish's spines.

227

Fishing a shingle beach

Shingle beaches offer a wide variety of fish to the angler. Cod, bass, dogfish, whiting, pouting, mackerel, dabs and thornback ray can all be taken in their seasons.

During favourable conditions a standard beachcaster, multiplier reel and a 3oz(90g) to 6oz(180g) lead will cope.

Strong winds, heavy seas and cross currents will demand the use of a back-casting rod and leads of 7oz (210g) or 8oz (240g).

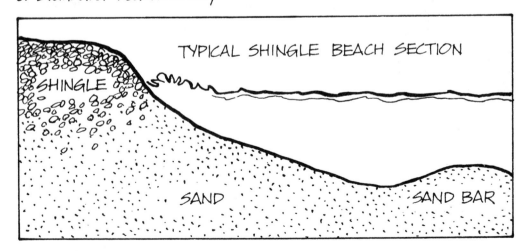

TYPICAL SHINGLE BEACH SECTION

SHINGLE

SAND

SAND BAR

Although not present all year round, cod are probably the most popular shingle beach quarry. During winter thousands of hardy anglers brave the elements, day and night, in their efforts to get to grips with a big cod.

Hotspots on a shingle beach

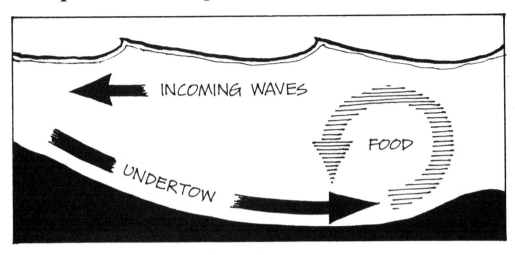

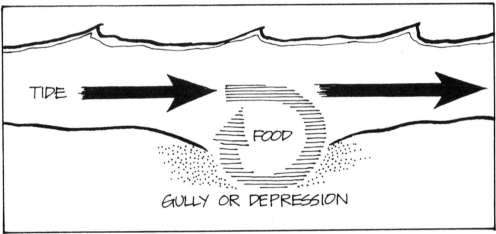

Unlike the storm beach angler, who has to leave his equipment well back from the advancing waves, the shingle beach fisherman can set up a base relatively close to the water. This is a great advantage to the winter cod angler who can prop his rod on a rest, shelter behind an umbrella, and still remain close to his rod should a bite occur.

There are a selection of rod rests available, but the type favoured by many experts is the one shown here which allows the rod to be propped at various angles.

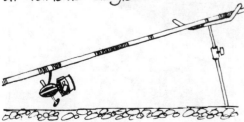

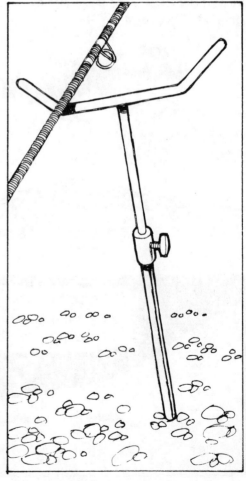

Cod

Cod feed predominantly close to the bottom, therefore a leger rig will account for the specimens.

Forged stainless hook, 4/0 to 6/0

15 lb (6·80 kg) to 20 lb (9·00 kg) trace

Bead

Swivel

Link swivel

Lead

Cod will grab just about any bait provided they are in a feeding mood — here are a few worth trying.

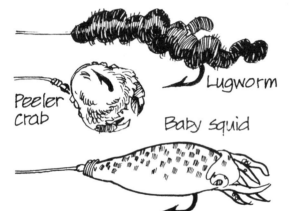

Lugworm

Peeler crab

Baby squid

Leave the hook-point and barb completely exposed.

Plain bombs roll along the sea-bed and come to rest in depressions, presenting the bait in a hotspot.

Night fishing usually produces the better fish.

A head lamp is invaluable when it comes to landing a cod during darkness. This item is not very expensive and can be obtained from most good tackle shops.

Very steeply-shelving beaches may present a problem when it comes to landing a big cod. This is when a companion comes to the rescue with a strong, long-handled landing net. It is always a good policy to be in the company of another angler when beach fishing after dark.

233

Dogfish

Dogfish hunt in packs over a broken sea-bed. Fishing at the extremities of a shingle beach, adjacent to a rocky promontory, will often bring the best results.

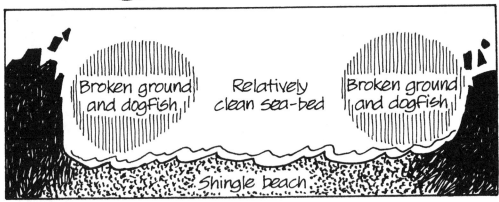

Broken ground and dogfish

Relatively clean sea-bed

Broken ground and dogfish

Shingle beach

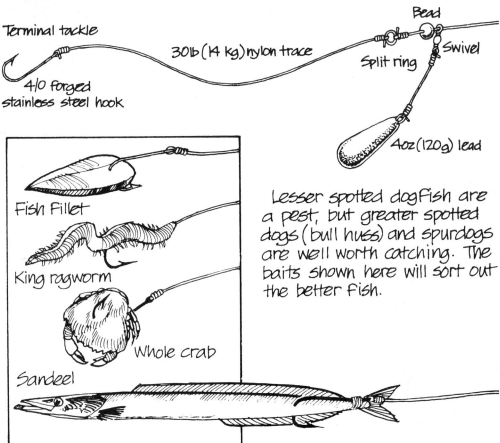

Terminal tackle

4/0 forged stainless steel hook

30lb (14 kg) nylon trace

Bead

Split ring

Swivel

4oz (120g) lead

Fish Fillet

King ragworm

Whole crab

Sandeel

Lesser spotted dogfish are a pest, but greater spotted dogs (bull huss) and spurdogs are well worth catching. The baits shown here will sort out the better fish.

Whiting

The best time to pursue this ravenous fish is at night, when it is possible to take fish in quick succession. During the winter they come close inshore and can be caught from all shingle beaches.

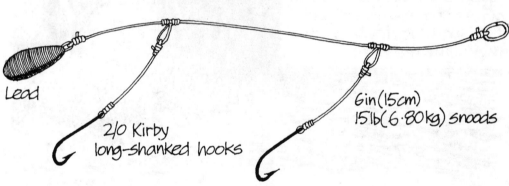

Lead

2/0 Kirby long-shanked hooks

6in (15cm) 15lb (6·80kg) snoods

BAITS

Mackerel or herring chunk

Lugworm/fish cocktail

Lugworm

235

Pouting

Like the whiting, the pouting feeds more freely after dark and will take any bait that is offered.

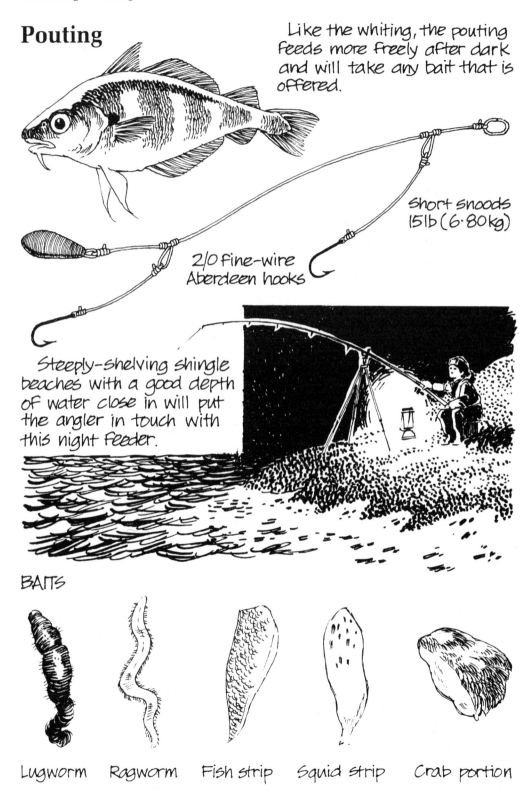

Short snoods
15lb (6·80kg)

2/0 fine-wire
Aberdeen hooks

Steeply-shelving shingle beaches with a good depth of water close in will put the angler in touch with this night feeder.

BAITS

| Lugworm | Ragworm | Fish strip | Squid strip | Crab portion |

236

Mackerel

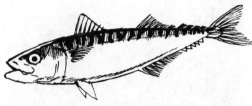

During the summer months mackerel chase small fry very close to the shoreline. Steeply-shelving beaches with a good depth of water will bring these predators within casting range of the angler.

A beachcasting rod is ideally suited to casting a team of feathers amongst the feeding mackerel.

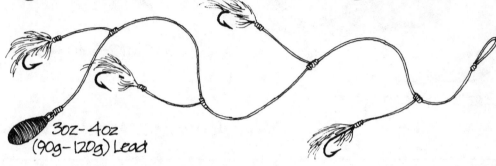

3oz–4oz (90g–120g) Lead

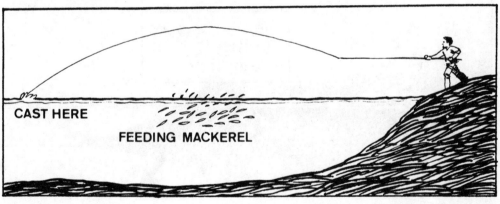

CAST HERE

FEEDING MACKEREL

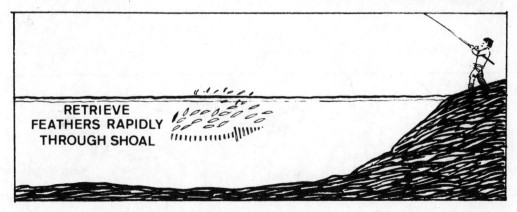

RETRIEVE FEATHERS RAPIDLY THROUGH SHOAL

237

Dabs

These are delightful little fish. They bite boldly and make excellent eating. Their favourite feeding grounds are over beds of hard-packed sand and shingle.

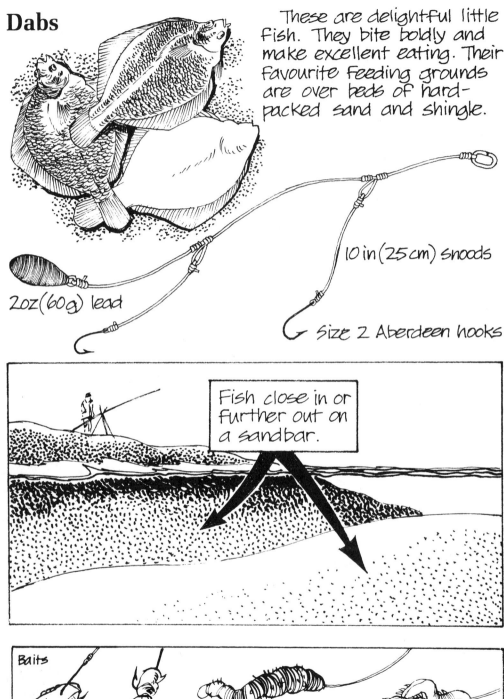

10 in (25 cm) snoods

2 oz (60 g) lead

Size 2 Aberdeen hooks

Fish close in or further out on a sandbar.

Baits

Peeler crab

Hermit crab

Lugworm

Ragworm

Thornback ray

A warm summer evening with a rising tide is the ideal combination for taking this bottom feeder.

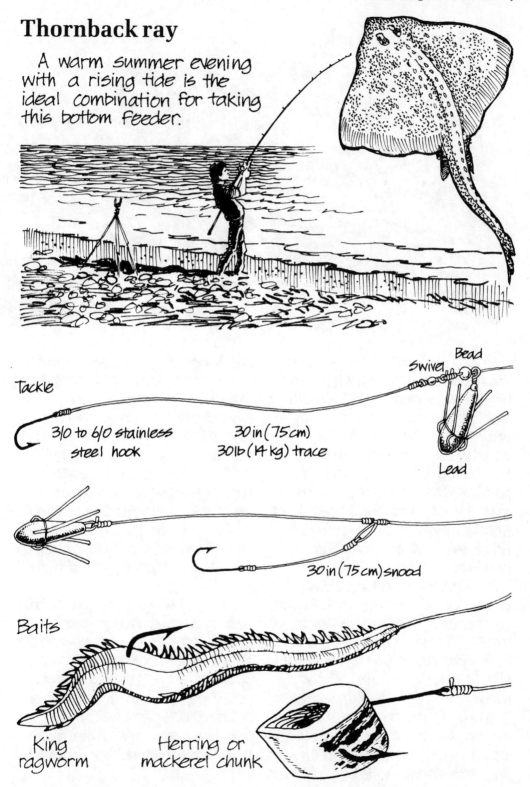

Tackle

3/0 to 6/0 stainless steel hook

30 in (75 cm) 30 lb (14 kg) trace

Swivel   Bead

Lead

30 in (75 cm) snood

Baits

King ragworm

Herring or mackerel chunk

Fishing from rocks

Rocks provide a haven for small creatures. Prawns, small fish, crabs and shellfish all shelter in the crevices and under the weed. These creatures form the diet of fish such as bass, conger, pollack and wrasse. As the tide flows and the water level creeps higher over the rocks food is flushed out and the predators feed.

A standard beachcasting rod is the ideal tool for rock fishing as the extra length permits more control over a hooked fish. It is advisable to step up the breaking strain of the main line when fishing rocky areas – abrasion from underwater rocks could result in a lost fish. However, lead links are best constructed of a lower breaking strain monofilament which will snap, under pressure, should the lead become snagged in a rock crevice. The main bulk of the terminal rig can then be retrieved intact. Where lead losses are high, old spark plugs can be used as a substitute weight.

There is seldom need to cast far from rocks – fish can often be caught directly beneath the rod tip.

As a safety precaution the angler should make sure that, at all stages of the tide, there is a way of exit to safe ground. It is also a good policy to inform a friend or relative of your fishing position and the time that you intend to return home.

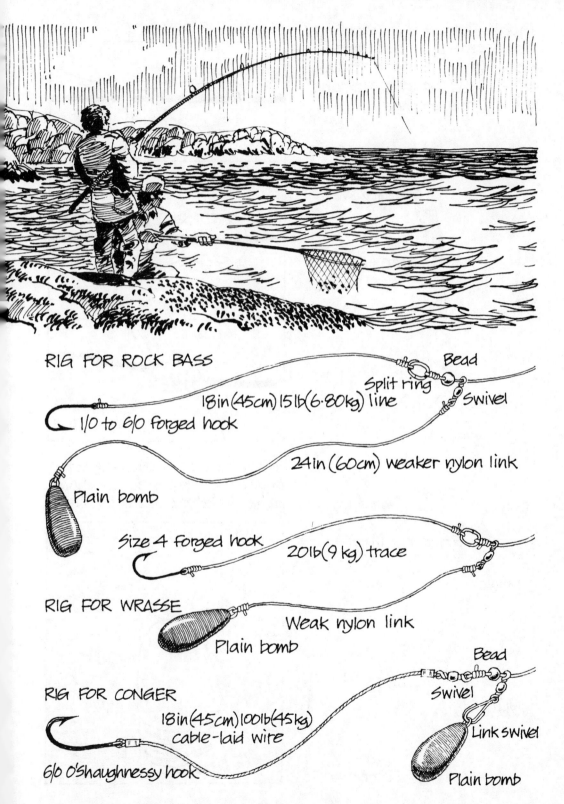

RIG FOR ROCK BASS

Bead

Split ring

18in (45cm) 15lb (6·80kg) line

Swivel

1/0 to 6/0 forged hook

24in (60cm) weaker nylon link

Plain bomb

Size 4 forged hook

20lb (9 kg) trace

RIG FOR WRASSE

Weak nylon link

Plain bomb

RIG FOR CONGER

Bead

18in (45cm) 100lb (45kg)
cable-laid wire

Swivel

Link swivel

6/0 O'Shaughnessy hook

Plain bomb

Float fishing is an ideal way of presenting a bait over a rock-littered bottom. Bass, wrasse and pollack respond well to this method.

FLOAT RIG

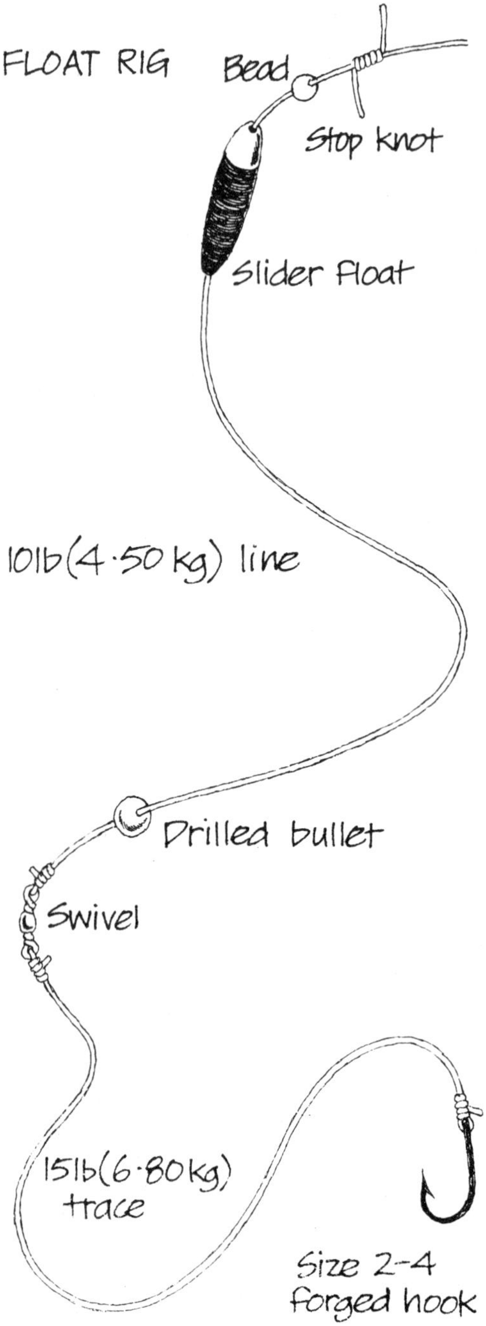

Bead

Stop knot

Slider float

10lb (4·50 kg) line

Drilled bullet

Swivel

15lb (6·80 kg) trace

Size 2-4 forged hook

SLIDING STOP KNOT

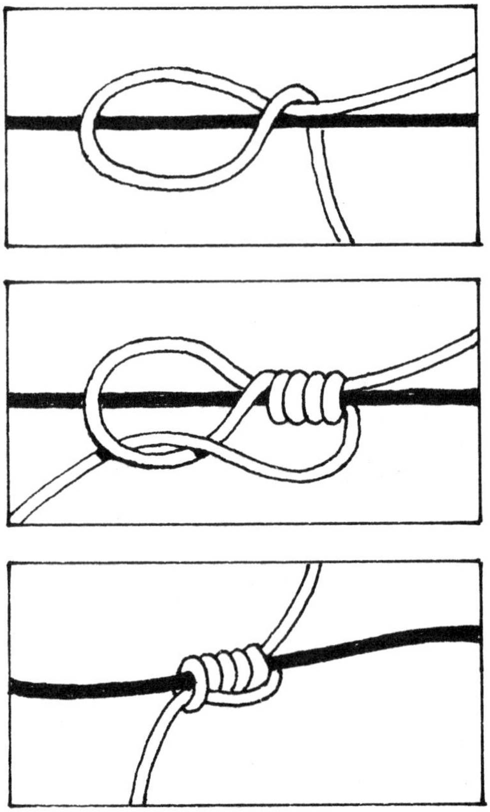

The tag ends of the knot should be trimmed to leave approximately ½in (12·7mm).

Bass

It is really surprising just how close in bass will be found when they are feeding around rocks. It is always an advantage if the angler is able to survey the proposed fishing spot during the low tide period in order to make a mental map of the area before it is covered by water.

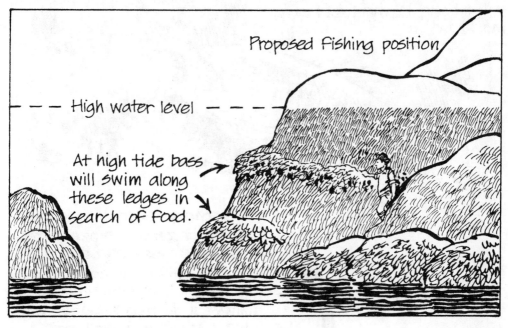

Proposed fishing position

High water level

At high tide bass will swim along these ledges in search of food.

Fish a float-fished bait over a ledge.

Rock bass will take a variety of float-fished baits such as peeler crab, ragworm, prawn or sandeel, but my favourite big-bass bait, especially in the proximity of a harbour, is the head of a mackerel.

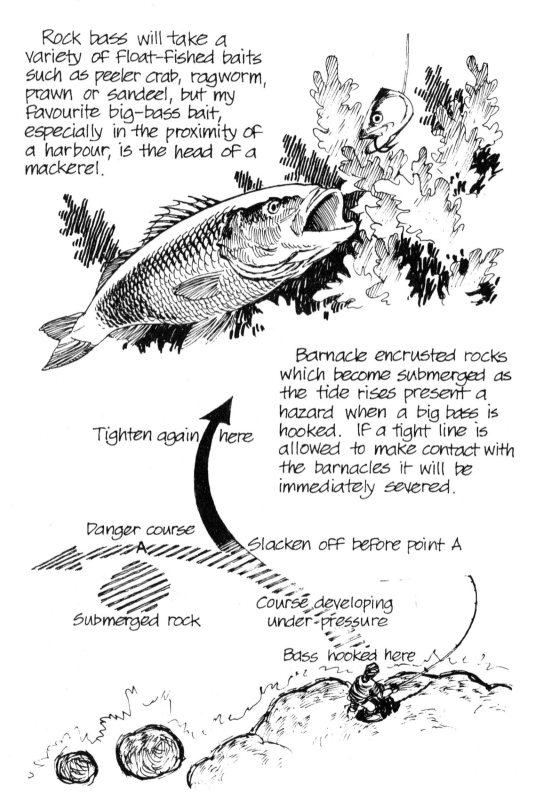

Barnacle encrusted rocks which become submerged as the tide rises present a hazard when a big bass is hooked. If a tight line is allowed to make contact with the barnacles it will be immediately severed.

Tighten again here

Danger course
A
Slacken off before point A

Submerged rock

Course developing under-pressure

Bass hooked here

Ballan wrasse

Although ballan wrasse can be caught on sliding float tackle, the best specimens are usually taken on bottom rigs. These larger fish live in deep, kelp-filled gullies.

Casting out to gullies is a chancy business. It is far better to select a fishing position which has a good depth of water at low tide and to fish virtually under the rod tip.

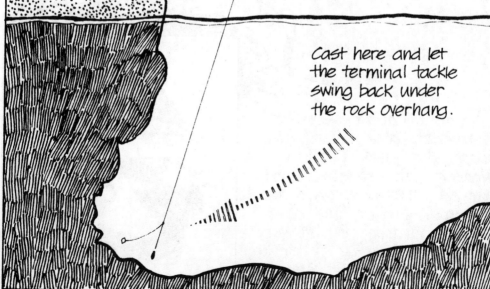

Cast here and let the terminal tackle swing back under the rock overhang.

245

Whole crab is definitely the best bait for big wrasse.

It is certainly an advantage to hold the rod while waiting for a bite. The extra length of a beachcasting rod coupled with a multiplier reel will provide more control over a hooked wrasse which has to be pulled out from the rock face.

A pair of artery forceps will be advisable for removing hooks. The jaws of a big wrasse can crunch a hard-backed crab in seconds and a human finger just as quickly. Wrasse are not very good to eat – far better to return them to the sea.

Pollack

Pollack also respond well to a float-fished bait. Set the float to fish the bait just clear of underwater rocks, cast out, and retrieve the tackle by slowly turning the reel handle.

A belly sliver of mackerel or a ragworm are the most effective baits for this sort of fishing.

A long-handled landing net is essential when landing large fish from rocks. Having a fishing companion present will make the landing operation much easier.

Conger

Wherever there are rocks there will be conger, especially if the rocks lie close to the entrance of a harbour. During the day conger tend to stay in their lairs, but during darkness they emerge and hunt for food. Therefore it is at night that the angler will stand the best chance of catching these eels. As they hunt mainly by scent, a fish bait will be most effective.

Cast the bait on to a clean area of sand, if one exists, close to rocks. Leave the reel in the free-spool position and engage the ratchet.

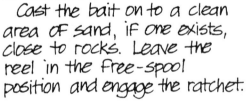

Bass

Bottom fishing for bass is best carried out in an area where fingers of rock exist, with sandy areas between.

The rod should be held whilst waiting for a bite. A fixed-spool or a multiplier reel are equally effective for this relatively close-in type of fishing. Ideal bait will be peeler crab, but during the autumn, when larger bass make an appearance, a dead pouting or mackerel bait will be effective. Cast the bait to lie alongside a rock finger.

Fishing an estuary

The beachcasting rod is well suited to fishing the waters of estuaries where long casts are often necessary.

A study of the estuary at low tide will reveal valuable features, such as the course of the main river channel or channels, the character of the bottom, and the type of creatures living thereon.

The average estuary will usually support colonies of lugworm in the mud just above low water mark, and crabs under weed-covered rocks. King ragworm might well exist if the foreshore is the right mixture of shale and mud. Smaller ragworms will probably be present on most venues.

This low-tide study provides the opportunity to collect these creatures for use as bait — peeler crabs are the bait par-excellence for most estuaries.

Professional bait diggers lay down lengths of drainage pipe or other objects to attract the moulting crabs. Such areas should be avoided, for to take advantage of them could result in an irate verbal onslaught from the bait digger.

Although bass can be caught on leger or paternoster rigs in most estuaries, the humble flounder seems to have more popularity, especially during the autumn and winter months.

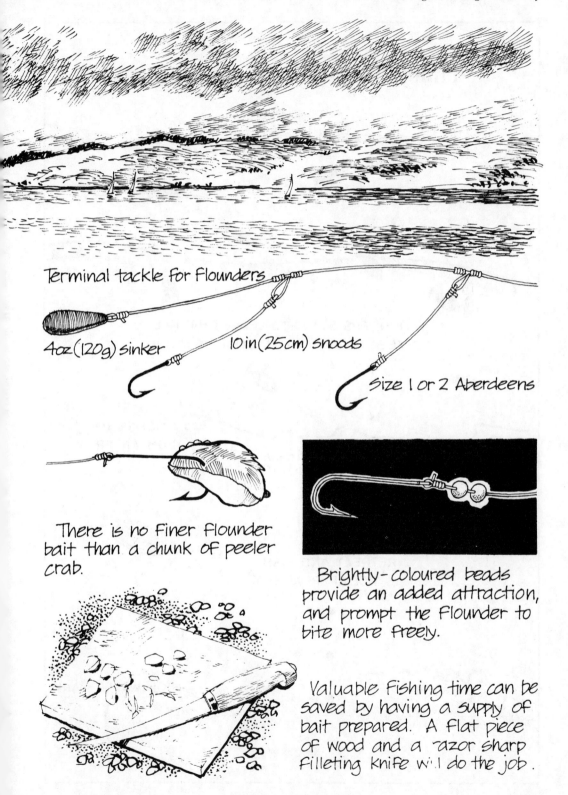

Terminal tackle for flounders

4oz (120g) sinker

10in (25cm) snoods

Size 1 or 2 Aberdeens

There is no finer flounder bait than a chunk of peeler crab.

Brightly-coloured beads provide an added attraction, and prompt the flounder to bite more freely.

Valuable fishing time can be saved by having a supply of bait prepared. A flat piece of wood and a razor sharp filleting knife will do the job.

251

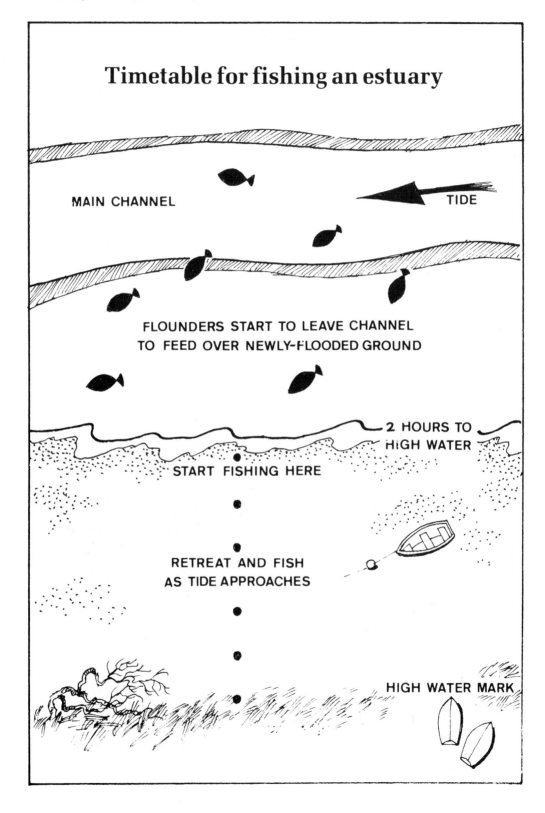

Timetable for fishing an estuary

MAIN CHANNEL

TIDE

FLOUNDERS START TO LEAVE CHANNEL
TO FEED OVER NEWLY-FLOODED GROUND

2 HOURS TO
HIGH WATER

START FISHING HERE

RETREAT AND FISH
AS TIDE APPROACHES

HIGH WATER MARK

As the water creeps up the shoreline the flounders will not be far behind and long casts could be over-shooting the mark. On many occasions a cast of 10 yds (9.15m) is enough to get amongst the fish.

Landing a flounder should pose no problems; they can be beached easily enough.

Sometimes, crabs are a bit thin on the ground, and running out of bait when the flounders are really on the feed can be very frustrating. By cracking open the legs of the crab the bait can be utilized to the full. Three or four legs threaded on to the hook makes a good bait.

Home-made casting leads

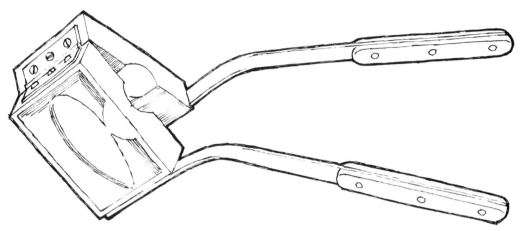

This method of making leads was kindly passed on to me by my friend Russ Symons, of Plymouth.

The advantage of using the converted mould, which is fitted with a hinge and a pair of handles, is that it allows the mould to be manipulated while it is still hot.

Converting the standard aluminium mould is a job for the experienced metal worker or engineer.

Pouring molten lead is a potentially dangerous procedure, if certain rules are not religiously followed, and should only be attempted under adult supervision.

rule 1

Cut the lead into small pieces, place in an old cast iron saucepan which has a pouring lip and heat until the lead is molten. Remove any floating rubbish with an old ladle.

Warm the mould over the heat source to disperse any moisture which may be present.

rule 2

Insert the loop, which can be the manufactured brass type with the serrated tag ends, or home-made from 18 guage stainless steel wire. If wire is used, splay the tag ends to achieve a better grip.

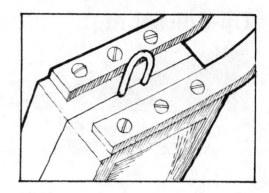

rule 3

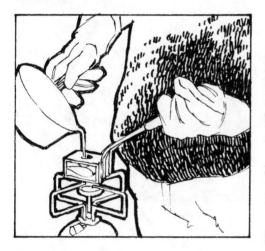

When pouring the lead, always wear heavy duty industrial gauntlets or gloves. Wear thick clothing, making sure that the arms are covered, and safety glasses goggles, or a full-face mask. Pour the lead very carefully, then replace the saucepan on the heater in readiness for the next pouring.

rule 4

Allow a few moments for the lead to solidify, then open the mould and give it a gentle tap to release the sinker. Insert a new loop and repeat the process while the mould is still hot.

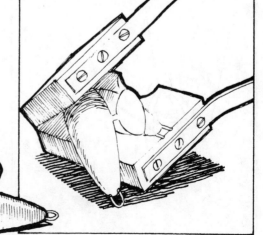

Up-tide fishing

This method is best suited to the comparatively shallow waters of estuaries, or over shallow, clean areas just offshore.

The bait—peeler, worm or fish—is cast up-tide from an anchored boat. Species caught by this method include bass, rays, flounders and plaice.

A paternoster is the best sort of terminal rig for up-tiding.

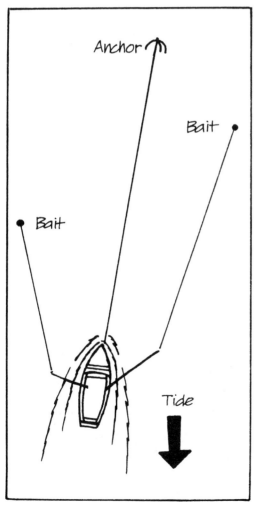

Anchor

Bait

Bait

Tide

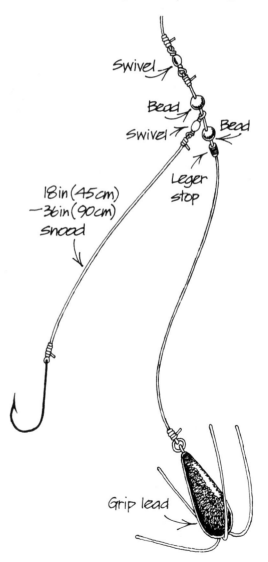

Swivel

Bead

Swivel

Bead

Leger stop

18in (45cm) —36in (90cm) snood

Grip lead

Fishing with the up-tide method is usually more productive than fishing over the stern of the boat, because noise and vibrations are carried, by the tide, away from the area where the bait is fished.

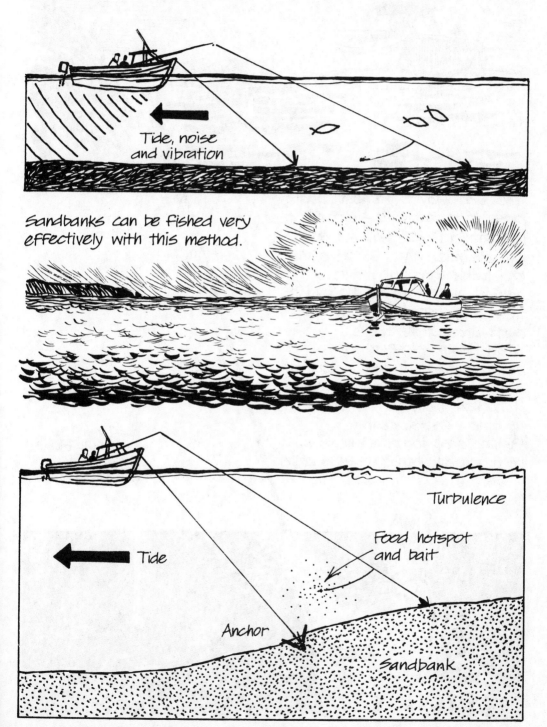

Tide, noise and vibration

Sandbanks can be fished very effectively with this method.

Turbulence

Food hotspot and bait

Tide

Anchor

Sandbank

Float fishing close to rocks

The ideal way to present a bait close to rocks is to suspend it beneath a float. This method will minimize the risk of losing end tackle, and will impart a natural movement to the bait as the tidal currents and eddies swirl around the rocks.

When fishing close to rocks it is an advantage to use a rod with a good length in order to control a hooked fish; the rod used for up-tide work is ideal.

Fishing close to rocks should only be practised when the sea is calm.

Stop knot

Sliding float
Swivel
Drilled bullet

Adjust the sliding stop knot to the deepest possible position, the idea being to present the bait (ragworm, crab or prawn) just clear of the rocks.

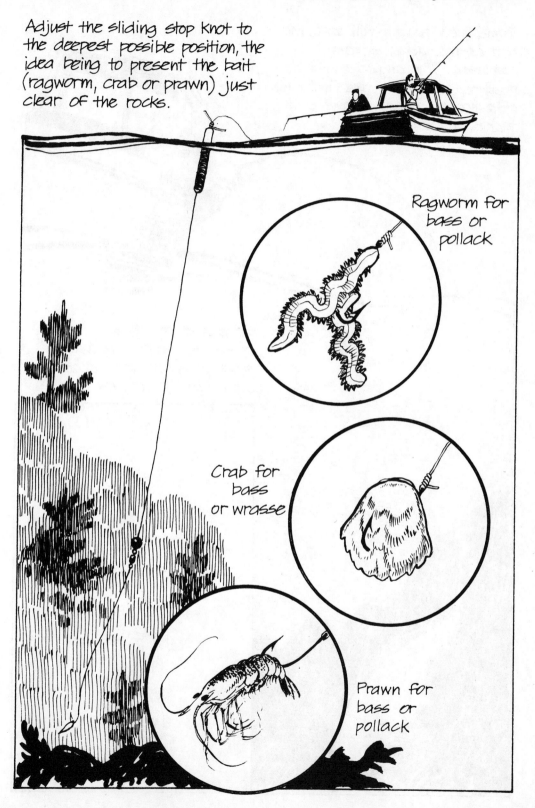

Ragworm for bass or pollack

Crab for bass or wrasse

Prawn for bass or pollack

Sometimes pollack will take the bait as the tackle is being retrieved. The angler should be prepared for this — the first rush of a hooked pollack tests both tackle and angler.

Some anglers attach a spoon or spinner above the bait in order to encourage pollack to strike on the retrieve.

Spinning over a reef

By cutting the engine, the boat is allowed to drift over the area of the reef. The lure is then cast, with the aid of a spinning rod, and allowed to sink to the required depth. It is then retrieved in a sink-and-draw motion. Bass are often caught this way, and pollack will also take a lure fished in this manner.

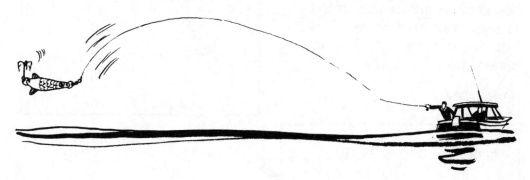

Cast here

— — — Sink
———— Retrieve

TOBY
For bass

LAURENS SPOON
For pollack

The paternoster

The paternoster is a versatile and invaluable rig to all boat anglers. The modern trend in paternosters is towards simplicity — moving away from the old designs, which often incorporated enough brass and steel wire booms almost to cause the boat to list.

BASIC NYLON
PATERNOSTER

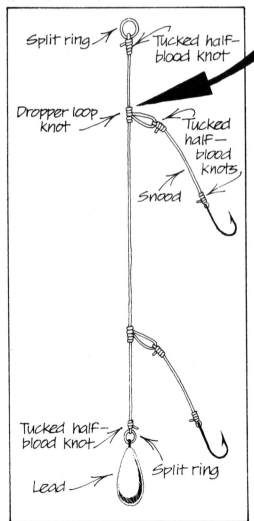

Some anglers incorporate ball-pen refill tubes as extra supports for the hook snoods.

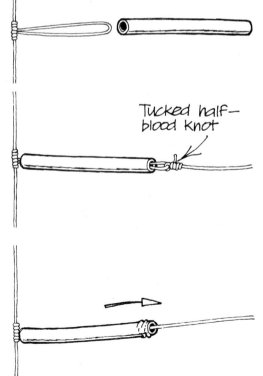

Paternoster with three-way swivels

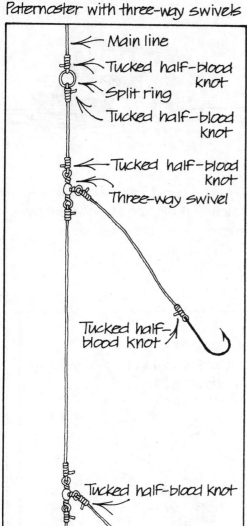

← Main line

Tucked half-blood knot

← Split ring

Tucked half-blood knot

← Tucked half-blood knot

Three-way swivel

Tucked half-blood knot →

Tucked half-blood knot →

Tucked half-blood knot

← Split ring

← Lead

Blood knot paternoster

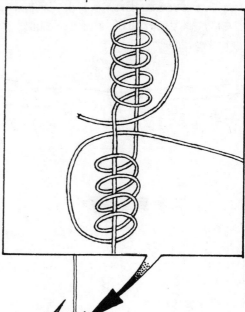

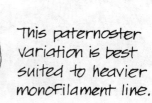

Trim end

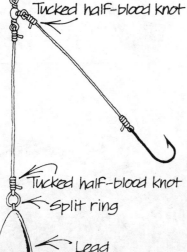

This paternoster variation is best suited to heavier monofilament line.

The paternoster is the perfect rig for presenting a bait, or baits, over rocky ground when fishing on the drift.

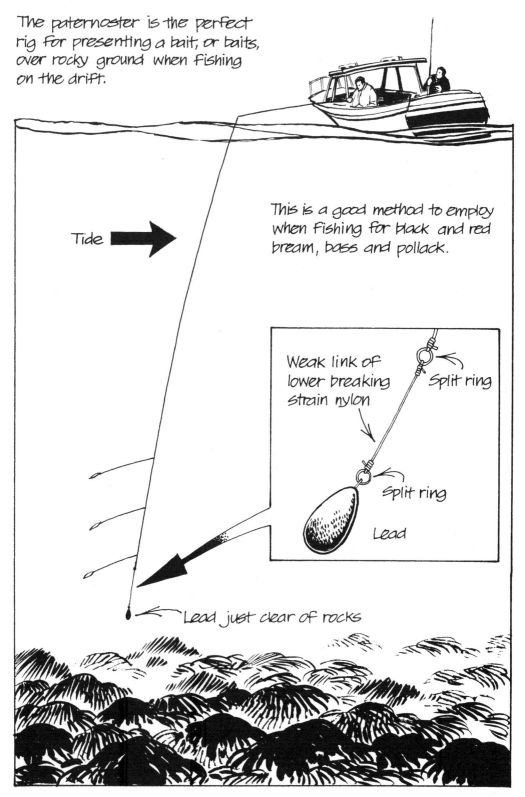

Tide

This is a good method to employ when fishing for black and red bream, bass and pollack.

Weak link of lower breaking strain nylon

Split ring

Split ring

Lead

Lead just clear of rocks

A 20lb (9 kg) class rod should be used with a two- or three-hook paternoster, for at times it is possible to hook two or even three fish at the same time.
A multiplier reel loaded with 18lb (8kg) line completes the outfit.

When the tide is slack, or during neap tides, it may be necessary to connect one or two wire booms.

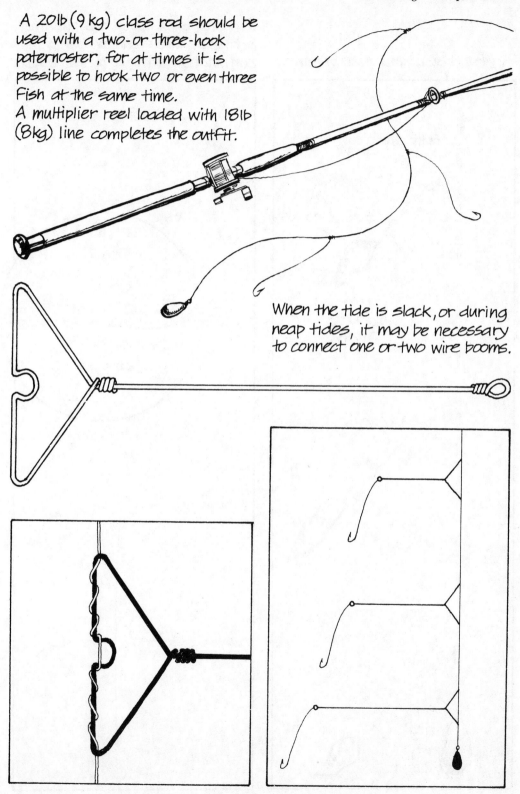

Rig for black and red bream.

If there is a good tide running, artificial lures can be used in conjunction with a paternoster.

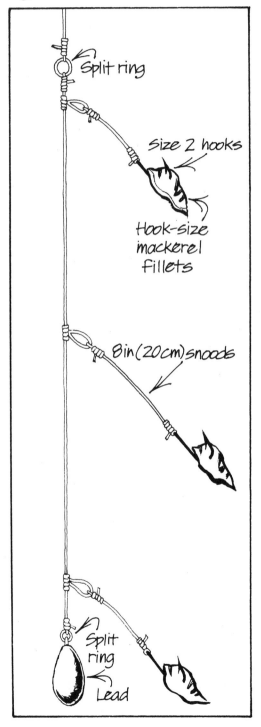

Split ring

Size 2 hooks

Hook-size mackerel fillets

8in (20cm) snoods

Split ring

Lead

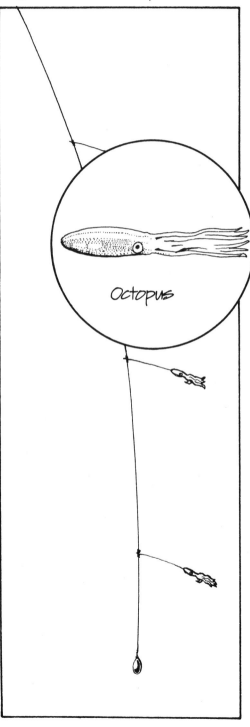

Octopus

Artificial lures tied to the ends of the snoods will attract predators, such as bass or pollack.

It is important to ensure that the snoods are spaced far enough apart to prevent tangles.

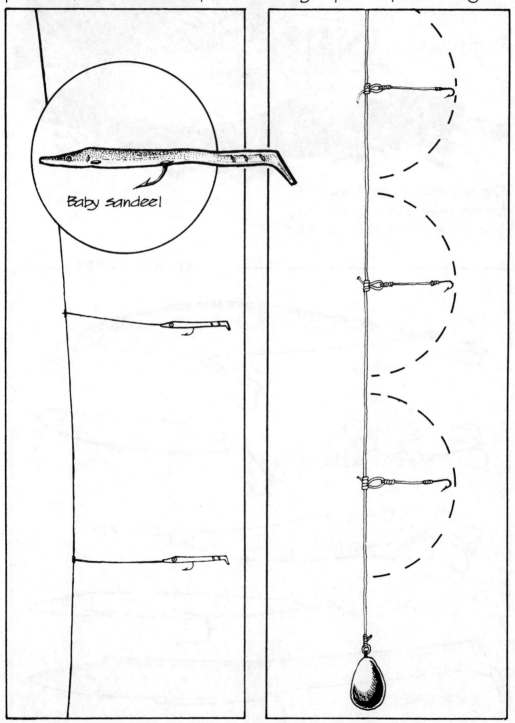

Baby sandeel

Fishing for bass

The most enjoyable way of
taking this bold and sporting
fish is with an artificial lure.

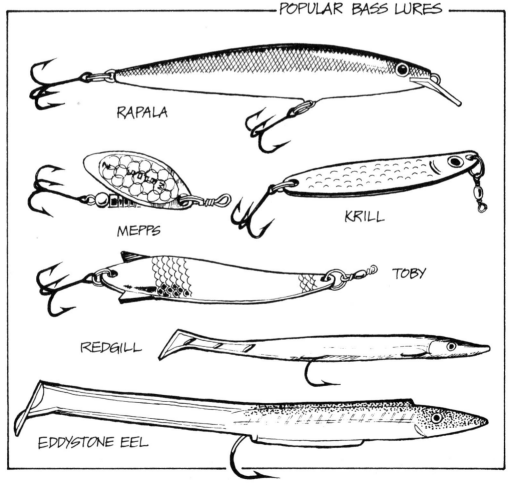

POPULAR BASS LURES

RAPALA

MEPPS

KRILL

TOBY

REDGILL

EDDYSTONE EEL

During the summer months, large shoals of small fry congregate and move close to the shoreline. Below the surface of the water bass take advantage of the easy pickings; above, seabirds such as terns and gulls have their share of the feast.

Keep a sharp look-out for birds wheeling and diving and steer the boat towards the disturbance. Proceed quietly and stop the boat well clear of the shoal.

269

Using a single-handed spinning rod, cast the lure beyond the area of fish activity.

By swinging the rod from side to side during the retrieve, a more natural action will be imparted to the lure, and it will then approach the boat in a zig-zag pattern, very typical of a wounded or panic-stricken bait fish.

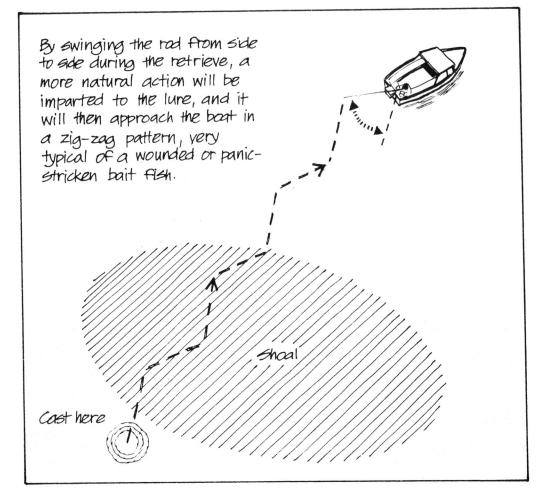

Shoal

Cast here

The majority of lures for this type of fishing are heavy enough in themselves, but extra weight may be needed for fishing artificial sandeels, or fishing at greater depth. This can be provided by using a foldover lead or a Wye lead.

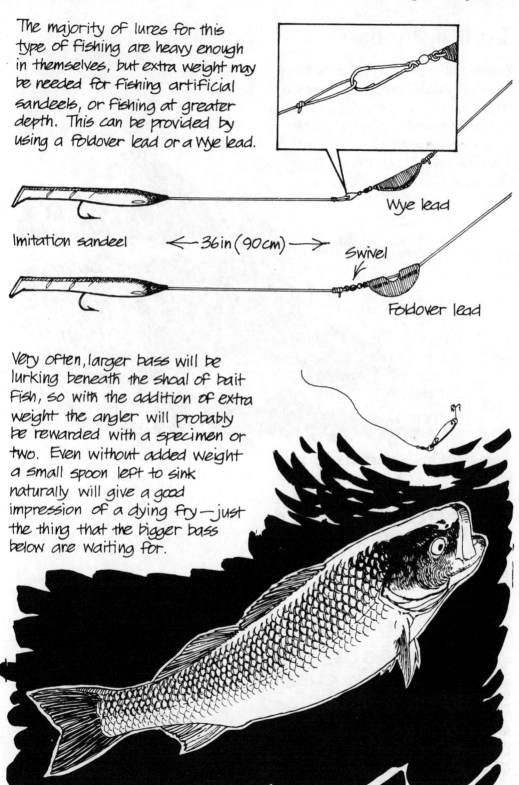

Imitation sandeel

←—36in (90cm)—→

Wye lead

Swivel

Foldover lead

Very often, larger bass will be lurking beneath the shoal of bait fish, so with the addition of extra weight the angler will probably be rewarded with a specimen or two. Even without added weight a small spoon left to sink naturally will give a good impression of a dying fry—just the thing that the bigger bass below are waiting for.

Trolling for bass

Bass will also be found lurking around jagged reefs. Reference to an Admiralty chart will disclose the whereabouts of such places, which sometimes rise from the seabed almost to the surface, and in some cases above it.

Reefs can be dangerous places for the inexperienced. The prudent angler, therefore, should always be in the company of someone who is conversant with the local rocks, and then only during settled weather conditions.

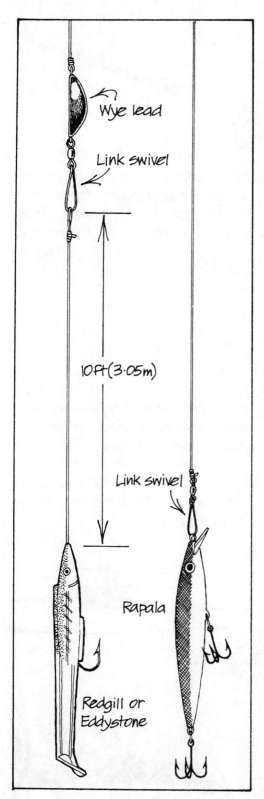

Wye lead

Link swivel

10ft(3·05m)

Link swivel

Rapala

Redgill or
Eddystone

Imitation sandeels and Rapala
lures are ideal for trolling. The
sandeel will need extra weight
to hold it down, but the Rapala
can be tied directly to the line.
The diving vane on the front of
the lure will cause it to dive.

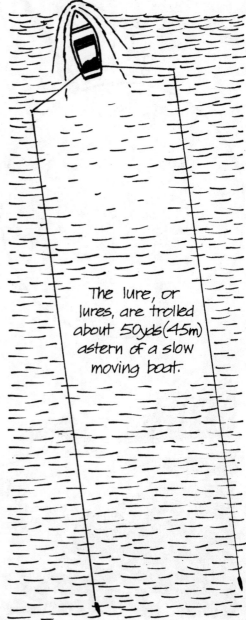

The lure, or
lures, are trolled
about 50yds(45m)
astern of a slow
moving boat.

The rod will need to be supported in some way during trolling until a fish hits the lure.

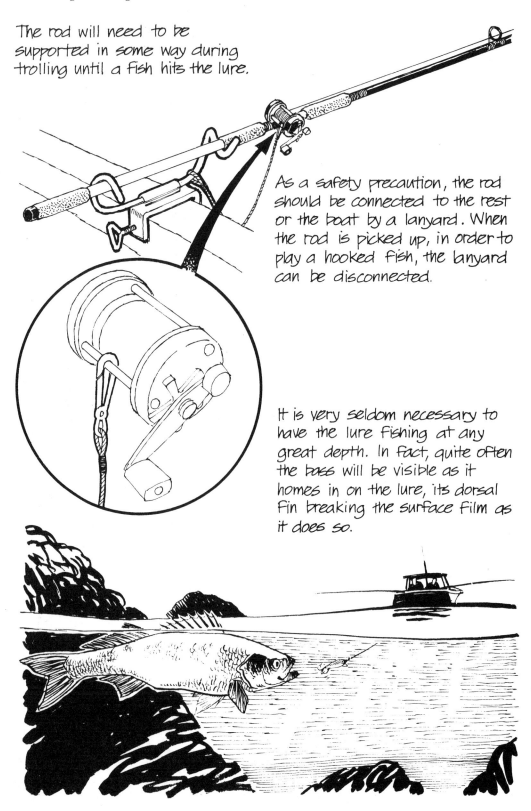

As a safety precaution, the rod should be connected to the rest or the boat by a lanyard. When the rod is picked up, in order to play a hooked fish, the lanyard can be disconnected.

It is very seldom necessary to have the lure fishing at any great depth. In fact, quite often the bass will be visible as it homes in on the lure, its dorsal fin breaking the surface film as it does so.

Driftlining for bass

This method is employed from a boat which is anchored up-tide of a sand bank. The bait most commonly used is a live sandeel.

Method for mounting sandeel

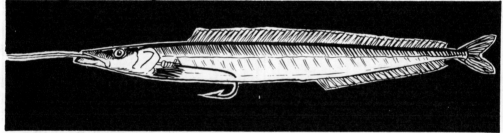

The best way of keeping sandeels alive and healthy is to put them in a wooden courge. The courge is then tethered to the boat by a lanyard and put into the water.

An alternative method is to put the sandeels in a bucket of fresh sea-water which has a battery-operated aerator attached.

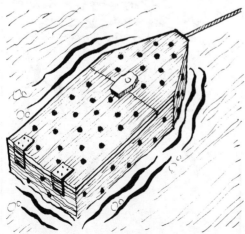

Some additional weight is usually required to hold the sandeel down, but this should be kept to a minimum to retain as natural a presentation as possible.

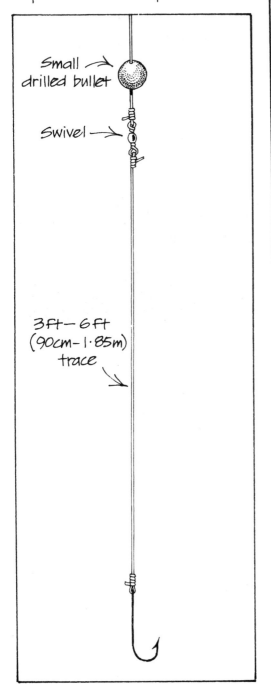

Small drilled bullet

Swivel

3ft — 6ft (90cm — 1.85m) trace

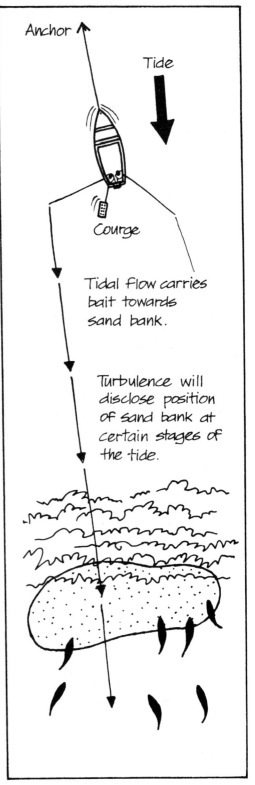

Anchor

Tide

Courge

Tidal flow carries bait towards sand bank.

Turbulence will disclose position of sand bank at certain stages of the tide.

Driftlining can be employed in many estuary mouths. The boat is allowed to drift with the tidal current, with the line and bait flowing out before the boat in a most natural manner.

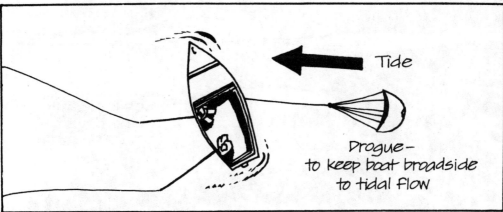

Tide

Drogue—
to keep boat broadside
to tidal flow

When a bass takes the bait, it should be given some slack line before the strike is made ....

.... then flick the reel into the 'on' position, pause for a second and lift the rod smoothly.

277

The driftline method can also be used to fish a prawn close to rocks. The prawn should be allowed to drift around naturally in the tidal eddies, therefore little or no lead will be required.

Fine wire Aberdeen hook

Prawns can be caught in a dropnet which is baited with scraps of fish. They can then be kept alive in a bucket of fresh sea-water which must be well oxygenated with an aerator pump.

How to catch prawns

Choose a spot with a snag—free bottom, with a fair depth of water, and close to rocks or a harbour wall. Lower the net to the bottom, wait for approximately five minutes, then draw the net quickly to the surface.

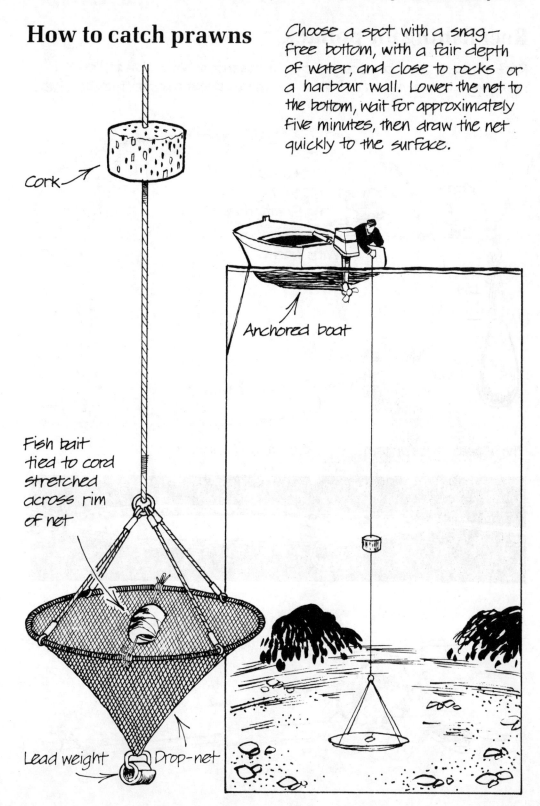

Cork

Fish bait tied to cord stretched across rim of net

Anchored boat

Lead weight   Drop-net

Reef fishing for pollack

Reef pollack can be caught by spinning, but a natural bait presented on a long, flowing trace is far more productive.

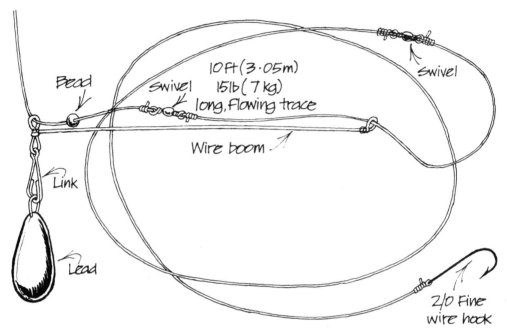

Bead

Swivel

10 ft (3.05m)
15 lb (7 kg)
long, flowing trace

Swivel

Wire boom

Link

Lead

2/0 Fine
wire hook

The finest bait for reef pollack is a live sandeel.

A 20 lb (9 kg) boat rod and a multiplier reel complete the outfit.

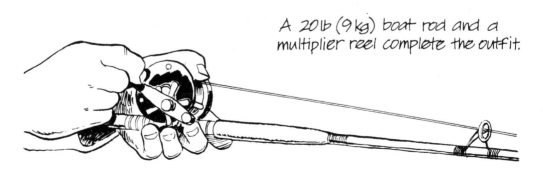

The terminal tackle is lowered, with the reel out of gear, until the lead hits the reef. The reel is then put into gear and the lead retrieved just clear of the rocks.

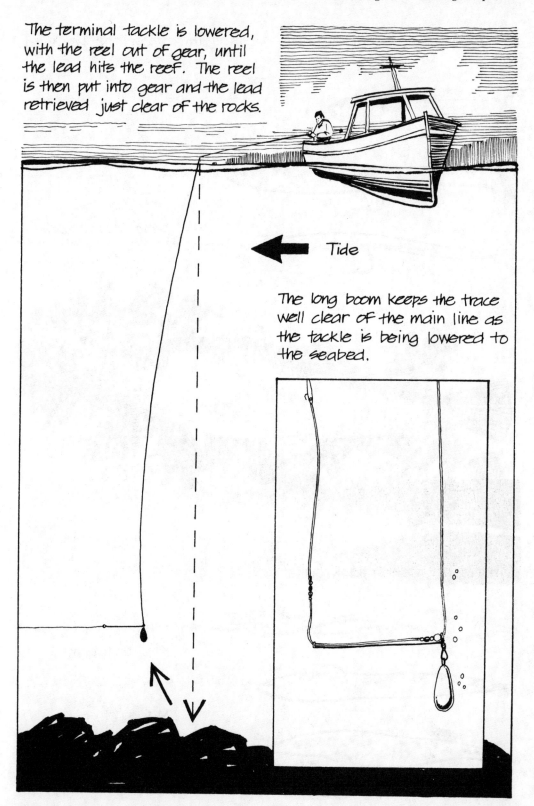

Tide

The long boom keeps the trace well clear of the main line as the tackle is being lowered to the seabed.

If live sandeel is not available a <u>small</u> imitation can be used.

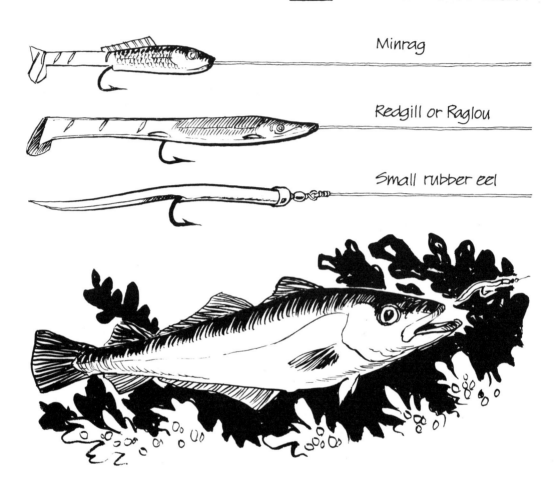

Minrag

Redgill or Raglou

Small rubber eel

Other good reef pollack baits

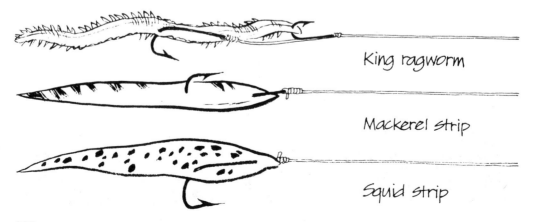

King ragworm

Mackerel strip

Squid strip

Fishing for ray

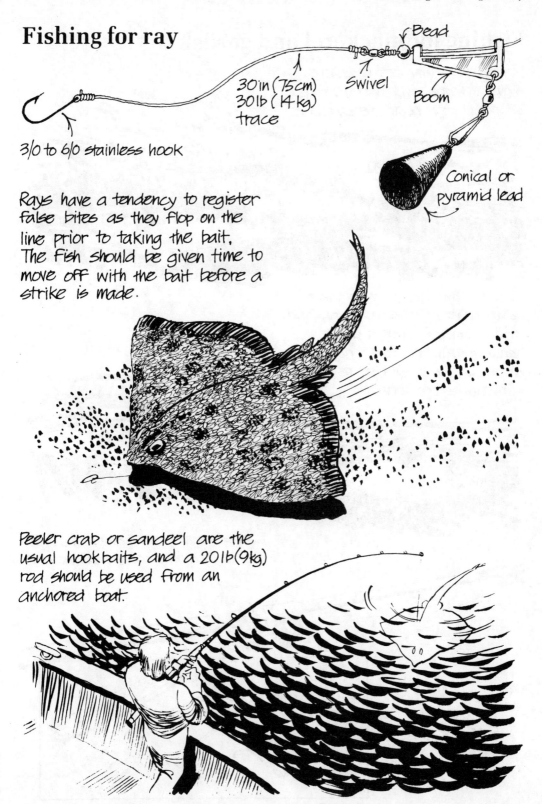

30 in (75cm)
30 lb (14 kg)
trace

Swivel

Bead

Boom

Conical or
pyramid lead

3/0 to 6/0 stainless hook

Rays have a tendency to register
false bites as they flop on the
line prior to taking the bait.
The fish should be given time to
move off with the bait before a
strike is made.

Peeler crab or sandeel are the
usual hookbaits, and a 20lb (9kg)
rod should be used from an
anchored boat.

283

Fishing for mackerel and garfish

During the summer, mackerel move inshore and harry shoals of small fry near the surface.

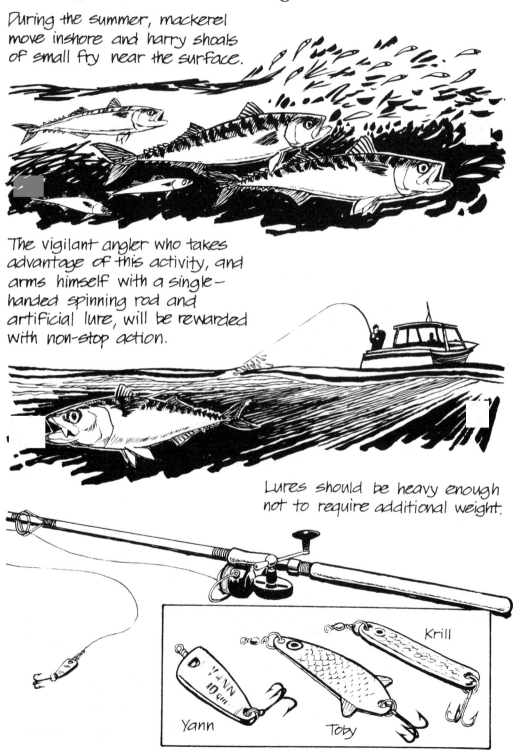

The vigilant angler who takes advantage of this activity, and arms himself with a single-handed spinning rod and artificial lure, will be rewarded with non-stop action.

Lures should be heavy enough not to require additional weight.

Yann

Toby

Krill

When a shoal of feeding mackerel is sighted, the boat should be manoeuvred to a position slightly in front of the shoal, and to one side. The engine should then be put into neutral gear and the boat allowed to drift.

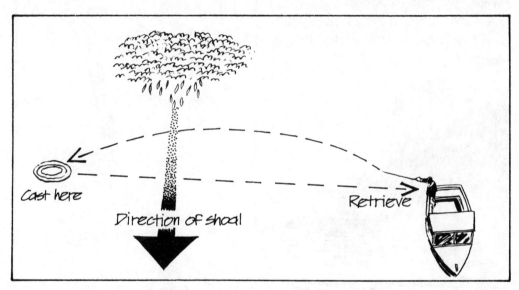

Cast here

Direction of shoal

Retrieve

The position of the boat will have to be adjusted every so often in order to keep in touch with the moving shoal. Never be tempted to take the boat too close to the shoal.

285

Mackerel also respond well to a float-fished bait, especially when it is fished in river mouths and harbours.

Simply let the tackle drift with the tide. It is a good policy to give the line a rub with line floatant.

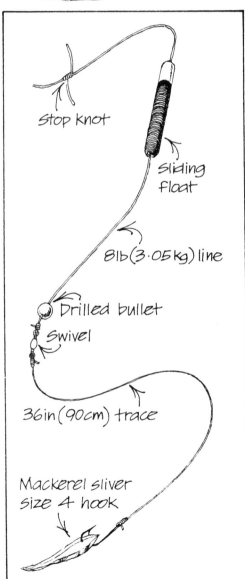

Stop knot

Sliding float

8lb (3·05 kg) line

Drilled bullet

Swivel

36in (90cm) trace

Mackerel sliver size 4 hook

A net containing fish offal, tied to the stern of the boat, will create a feed lane through which to trot the float tackle.

Check the passage of the float occasionally to impart a little more attraction to the bait.

After each trot down-tide, the tackle should be retrieved very slowly — fish often take the bait at this stage.

Rigs for mackerel trolling

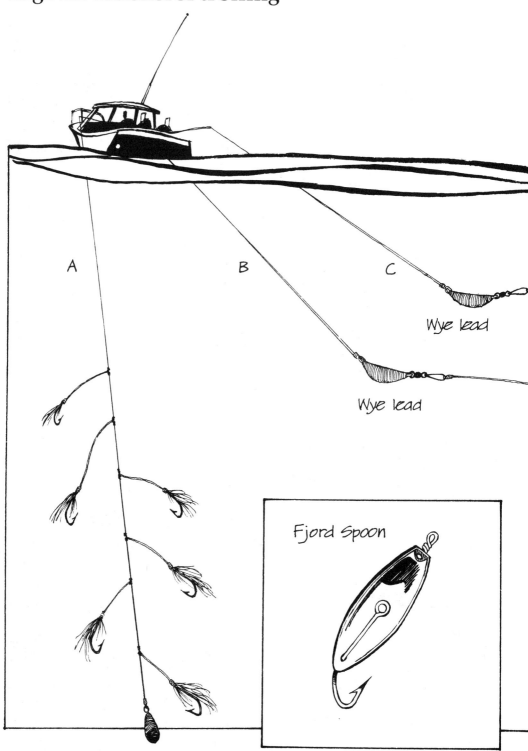

A

B

C

Wye lead

Wye lead

Fjord Spoon

Rig (A) is the same set-up as that used for jigging feathers under a drifting boat. Spoons or spinners can be substituted for the feathers. This rig should be trolled very slowly in order to keep the feathers or spoons fishing at a decent angle from the line.

Rigs (B) and (C) are more suited to shallower water and should be trolled about 50 yds (45 m) astern of the boat.

Handlines are often used for this method of catching mackerel although more often by the casual holiday-maker than by the serious angler.

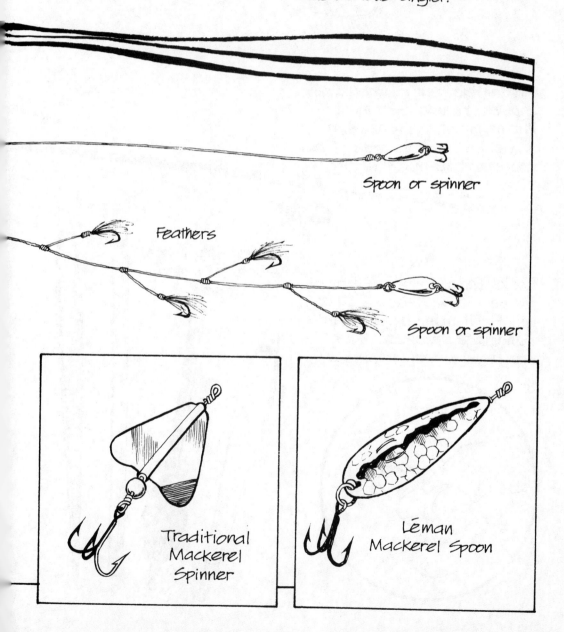

Spoon or spinner

Feathers

Spoon or spinner

Traditional Mackerel Spinner

Léman Mackerel Spoon

Fishing for grey mullet

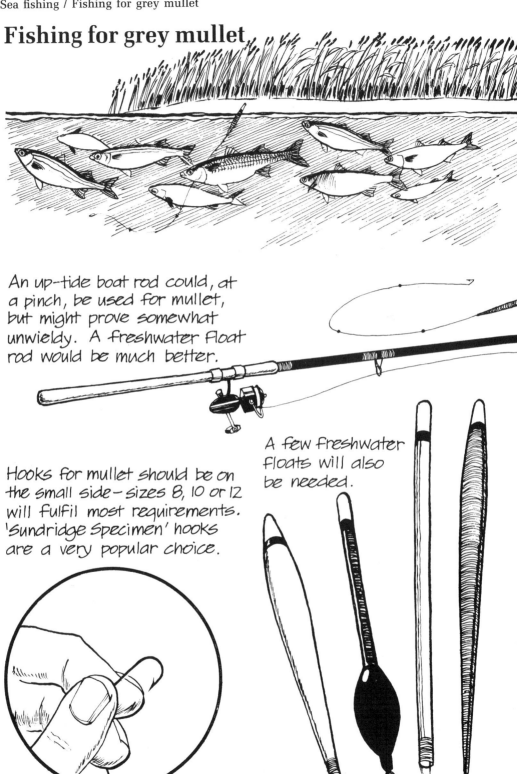

An up-tide boat rod could, at a pinch, be used for mullet, but might prove somewhat unwieldy. A freshwater float rod would be much better.

Hooks for mullet should be on the small side — sizes 8, 10 or 12 will fulfil most requirements. 'Sundridge Specimen' hooks are a very popular choice.

A few freshwater floats will also be needed.

The best areas in which to look for grey mullet are estuaries, harbours and salt-water lagoons. Shoals will move into these areas as the tide starts to flow.

The best plan of attack is to position the boat on a known mullet route just before the tide starts to flow.

Mullet will take a variety of baits.

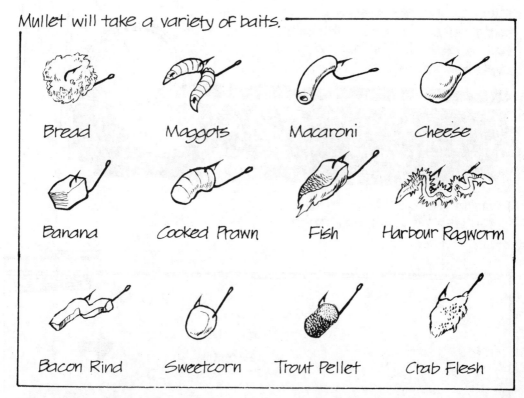

Bread   Maggots   Macaroni   Cheese

Banana   Cooked Prawn   Fish   Harbour Ragworm

Bacon Rind   Sweetcorn   Trout Pellet   Crab Flesh

Pilchard oil makes an ideal additive to most baits and loose feed.

No matter what bait the mullet angler decides to use, its effect will be enhanced by the intro—duction of a certain amount of free offerings identical to the hook bait. A meshed bag hanging under the boat, and filled with necessary samples, will ensure a constant stream of loose feed.

Maggots are best dispensed by putting them in a tin which has had holes drilled in the sides and bottom.

Float tackle is allowed to follow the tidal flow amidst the particles of loose feed.

Tide

There is no hard and fast rule on when to strike a mullet bite. These fish are wizards at playing with the bait, and will often nudge it with their top lip without actually taking it in their mouth.

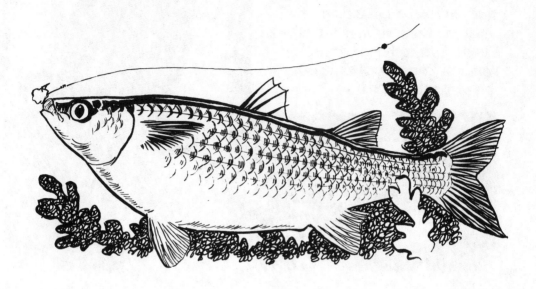

In order to keep in touch with the shoal the anchor will have to be lifted at intervals, this will allow the boat to drift up-tide.

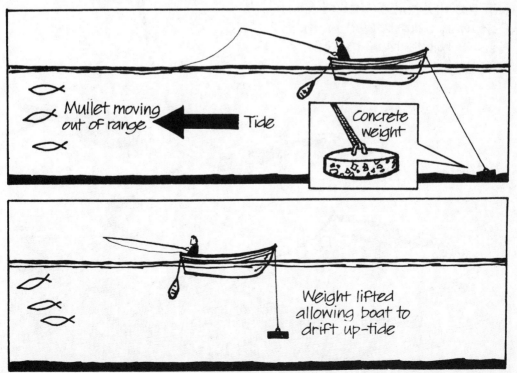

Mullet moving out of range

Tide

Concrete weight

Weight lifted allowing boat to drift up-tide

Harbours do not present as
many problems as open estuaries.
The mullet tend to stay in one
area through the duration of the
tide, so there is seldom any
need to keep moving the boat.
Mullet love to hang around
beneath cargo boats, waiting
for scraps of food.

A slow-sinking bait with most, or
all, of the weight near the float
will usually tempt these harbour
fish, which are bolder in their
feeding habits than the fish of
the estuary.

In some areas mullet are quite predatory and will attack a small spoon, especially if it is baited with harbour ragworm.

A piece of floating bread crust fished free-line, or with just a small section of peacock quill held to the line by float rubbers will also tempt mullet.

Whichever method is used to capture these powerful fish, a landing net is essential, and should always be close at hand.

Turbot and brill

Banks of sand, shell-grit or gravel provide the ideal habitat for these much sought-after species.

A 20lb (9kg) class rod is used in conjunction with a multiplier reel loaded with 18lb (8kg) line.

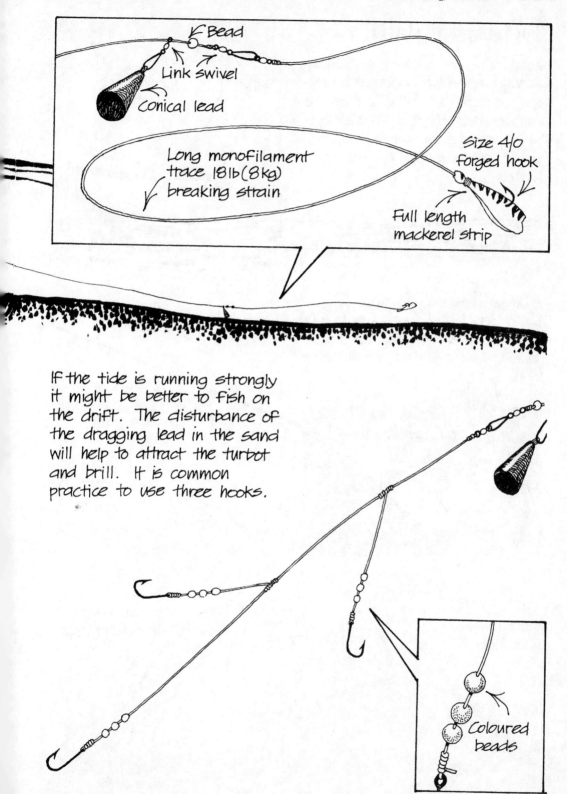

Bead

Link swivel

Conical lead

Long monofilament
trace 18 lb (8 kg)
breaking strain

Size 4/0
forged hook

Full length
mackerel strip

If the tide is running strongly
it might be better to fish on
the drift. The disturbance of
the dragging lead in the sand
will help to attract the turbot
and brill. It is common
practice to use three hooks.

Coloured
beads

Fishing for dabs

Dabs make delicious eating and provide non-stop action if a hot-spot is located. Very light tackle can be used for this little fish, which can be caught in shallow water, often directly under the boat.

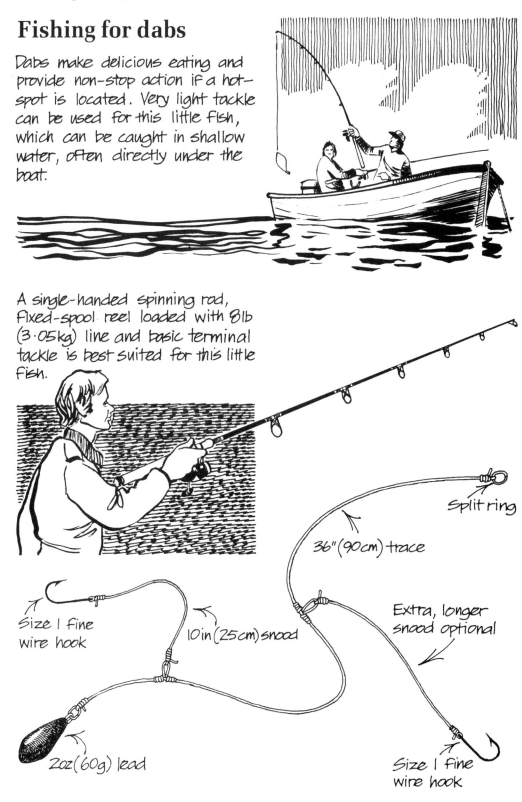

A single-handed spinning rod, fixed-spool reel loaded with 8lb (3·05kg) line and basic terminal tackle is best suited for this little fish.

Split ring

36" (90cm) trace

Size 1 fine wire hook

10in (25cm) snood

Extra, longer snood optional

2oz (60g) lead

Size 1 fine wire hook

The prime bait for dabs is peeler crab, which should be cut into sections to provide neat, small hook baits.

By cracking the shell on the claws and legs, the flesh can be removed to make the bait supply last longer.

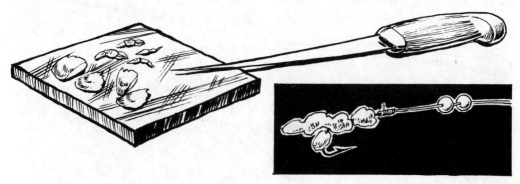

Dabs like a clean, sandy bottom, preferably on the slopes of a sandbank. Neap tides provide the ideal conditions for this sweet-tasting little fish.

Coloured beads set above the hook create an extra attraction.

Sole are also, occasionally, taken with this tackle, especially if the fishing is being carried out after dark.

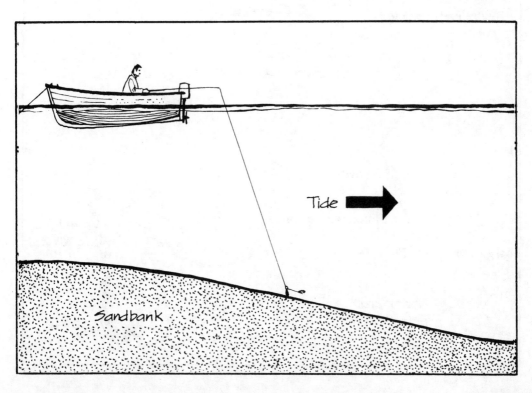

Tide

Sandbank

Fishing for flounders and plaice

Flounders are far more common than plaice but often share the same feeding grounds. Tackle can be identical for both species.

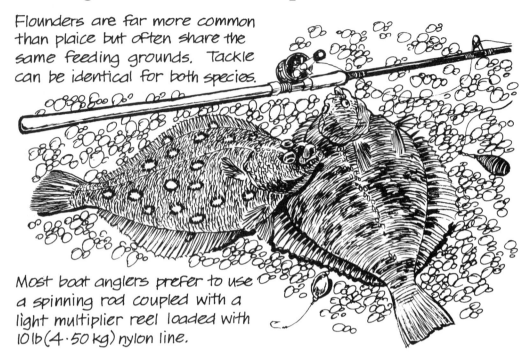

Most boat anglers prefer to use a spinning rod coupled with a light multiplier reel loaded with 10 lb (4·50 kg) nylon line.

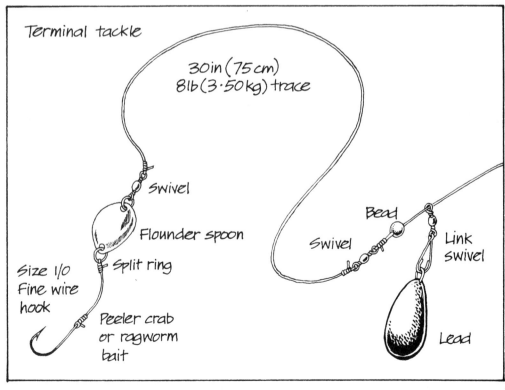

Terminal tackle

30 in (75 cm)
8 lb (3·50 kg) trace

Swivel

Flounder spoon

Size 1/0
Fine wire
hook

Split ring

Peeler crab
or ragworm
bait

Swivel

Bead

Link
swivel

Lead

Three ways of using the rig.

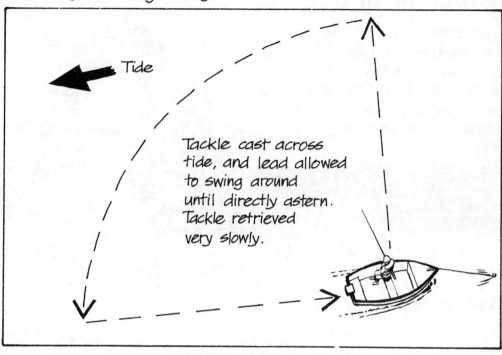

Tide

Tackle cast across tide, and lead allowed to swing around until directly astern. Tackle retrieved very slowly.

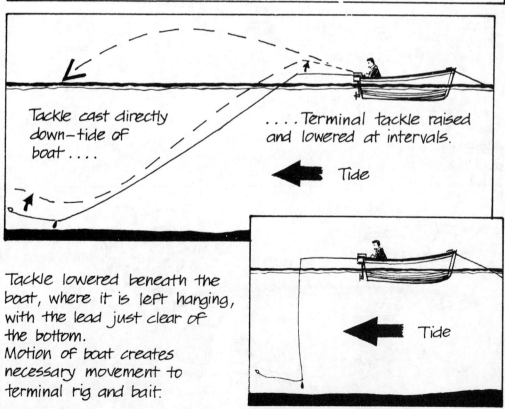

Tackle cast directly down-tide of boat . . . .

. . . . Terminal tackle raised and lowered at intervals.

Tide

Tackle lowered beneath the boat, where it is left hanging, with the lead just clear of the bottom.
Motion of boat creates necessary movement to terminal rig and bait.

Tide

Fishing for dogfish

This scavenger hunts in packs, and sport can be fast and furious if a concentration of the species is located. They feed mainly over rough ground, where the angler should present the bait right on the bottom.

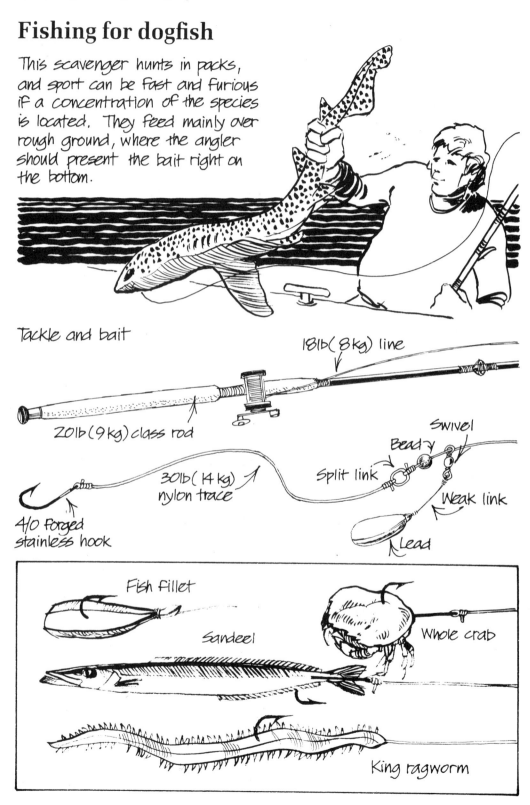

Tackle and bait

18lb (8kg) line

20lb (9kg) class rod

Swivel

Bead

Split link

Weak link

30lb (14kg) nylon trace

4/0 forged stainless hook

Lead

Fish fillet

Sandeel

Whole crab

King ragworm

The best time for 'dogs' is after dark or during poor light.

Remember! The dogfish is related to the shark family and the skin is very rough. Always wear a thick leather glove when handling these fish.

Large dogfish can weigh as much as 15lb (7kg).

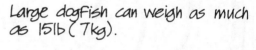

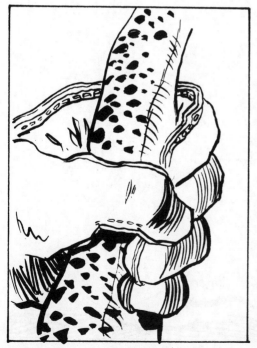

Wreck fishing

Fishing over a deep-water wreck
will require a bigger financial outlay
than inshore fishing, but will produce
larger than average specimens. 30lb
(14 kg) line will be needed, coupled
with a 33lb (15 kg) class rod.

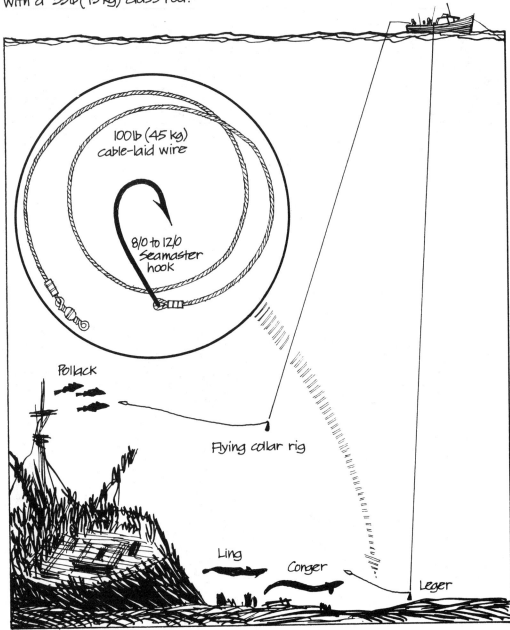

100lb (45 kg)
cable-laid wire

8/0 to 12/0
Seamaster
hook

Pollack

Flying collar rig

Ling

Conger

Leger

Wreck fishing

Fishing with a pirk is becoming increasingly popular with wreck fishermen, and accounts for many jumbo-sized cod.

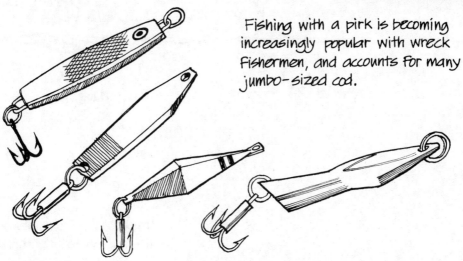

The pirk is lowered to the required depth, then worked up and down by raising and lowering the rod. This produces an attractive, fluttering action which is irresistible to big predators.

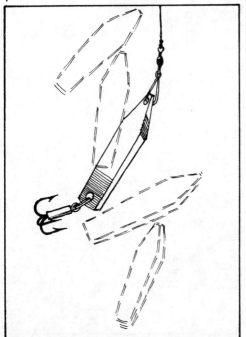

Variation on a pirk theme.

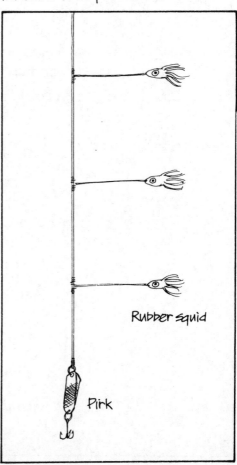

Rubber squid

Pirk

305

Shark fishing

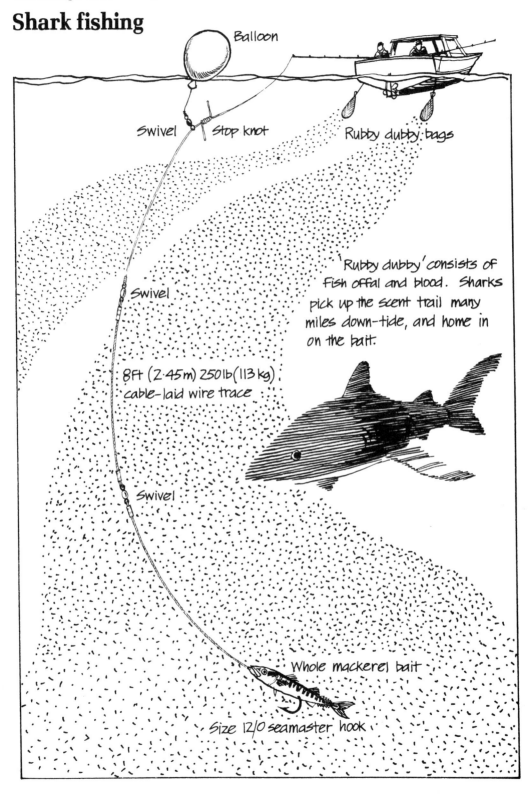

Balloon

Swivel   Stop knot

Rubby dubby bags

'Rubby dubby' consists of fish offal and blood. Sharks pick up the scent trail many miles down-tide, and home in on the bait.

Swivel

8ft (2·45m) 250lb (113kg) cable-laid wire trace

Swivel

Whole mackerel bait

Size 12/0 seamaster hook

Playing a fish

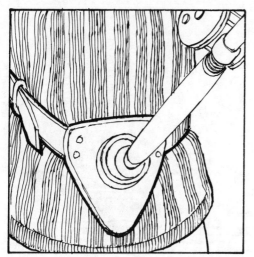

Bringing a heavy fish up through several fathoms of water puts a strain on both angler and tackle.

To protect the angler's groin, a special butt pad is worn.

With the brake on the reel in the 'on' position, and the drag set to the highest possible tension, subject to the breaking strain of the line, the rod is lifted hard into the fish.

The rod is then lowered, and at the same time line is retrieved onto the spool.

Once again the rod is lifted, and the same operation is repeated until the fish arrives at the surface.

Pinpointing a mark

If a good fishing spot has been located in sight of land, the angler will, no doubt, wish to return at some other date, to enjoy further sport. Providing there are recognizable landmarks, this should be an easy matter of taking a couple of bearings.

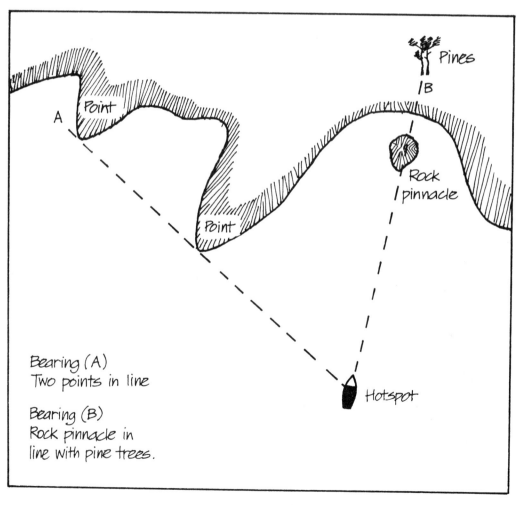

Pines

B

Point

A

Point

Rock
pinnacle

Hotspot

Bearing (A)
Two points in line

Bearing (B)
Rock pinnacle in
line with pine trees.

Safety in the boat

Even in the comparatively sheltered waters encountered by the inshore boat angler, the sea can often be a very fickle and dangerous place. Every angler should be prepared for any emergency by making sure, before putting to sea, that all the items shown here are on board.

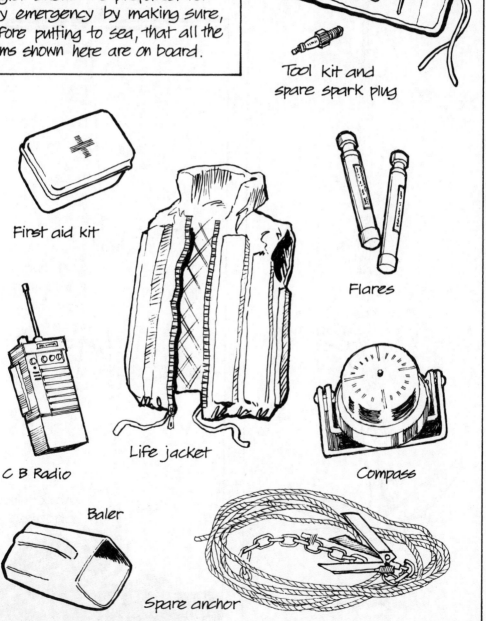

Tool kit and spare spark plug

First aid kit

Flares

C B Radio

Life jacket

Compass

Baler

Spare anchor

When fishing from a small craft it is advisable to 'trip' the anchor, so that in the event of the anchor jamming in rocks it can be pulled free.

Remain seated and pull from the bows.

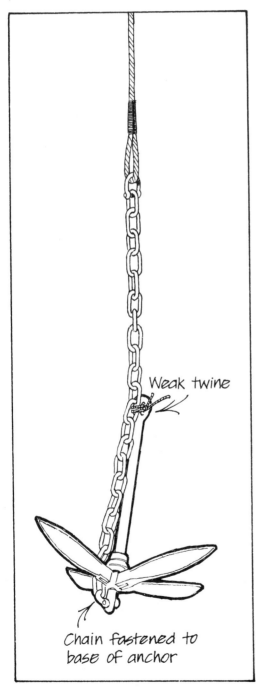

Weak twine

Chain fastened to base of anchor

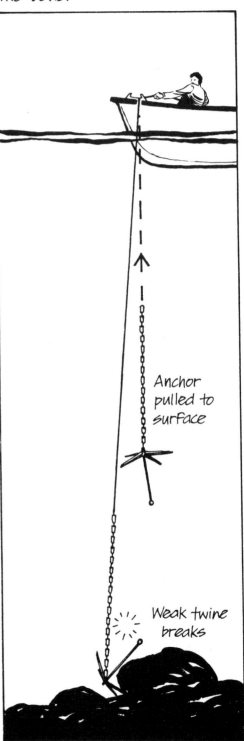

Anchor pulled to surface

Weak twine breaks

Clothing

Even in summer it can feel cold onboard a boat. This can be miserable, and definitely affects concentration and efficient angling.

Exposed beaches can be the most soul-destroying places if you are not equipped with sufficient clothing. You can always shed clothing if you become too warm. You cannot conjure up extra layers when you have not taken enough.

ITEMS
Boat angler— woolly hat, polo-neck sweater, pvc jacket with hood, waterproof over-trousers, rope-soled yachting shoes.
Beach angler— woolly hat, polo-neck sweater, waxed or pvc jacket and hood, waders.

Boat angler

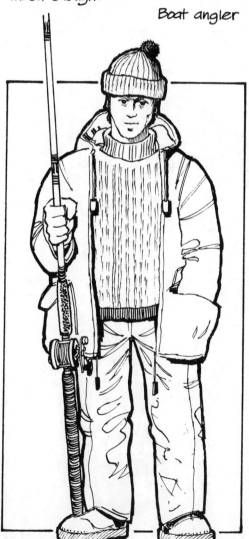

Beach angler

Accessories

KNIFE
This is an essential piece of equipment both for filleting fish and for cutting up fish and crab baits. It should be kept razor-sharp at all times.

TACKLE BOX
For containing small items of tackle in an orderly fashion. Most boxes nowadays are plastic, which is non-corrosive, but the fittings are metal and will need to be treated every so often with water repellant spray and oil.

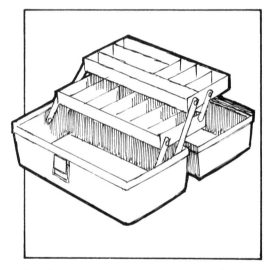

PRESSURE LAMP
There are quite a few different types to choose from. They all provide a good light, necessary for beach fishing after dark, and a source of heat for cold fingers.

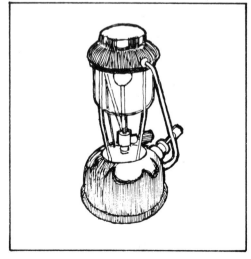

Accessories

HOOK SHARPENING STONE
When fishing over rough ground, hooks are liable to lose their sharpness very quickly. Check the hook before every cast, and if it is blunt use the stone. If the hook is damaged, tie on a new one.

UMBRELLA
This piece of equipment is usually associated with the fresh-water fishing scene, but is just as necessary on a wet and windswept beach, for keeping the angler and his equipment dry.

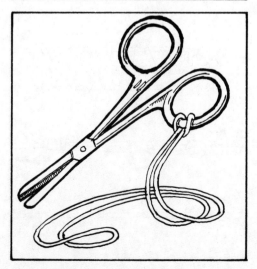

ARTERY FORCEPS
When buying forceps for sea fishing, make sure that they are made from stainless steel. Keep them close at hand for extracting hooks from fish. The best way to do this is to fasten them to a lanyard and hang them around your neck.

Knots

TUCKED FULL BLOOD KNOT
For joining line of widely-differing thickness. The thinner line must be doubled at the tying end, and taken around the thicker line twice as many times as the thicker line is turned around it.

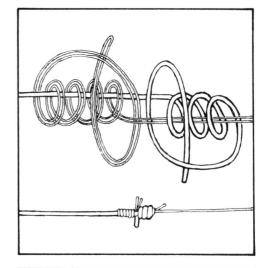

PALOMAR KNOT
A simple, neat and efficient knot for connecting a hook to nylon line.

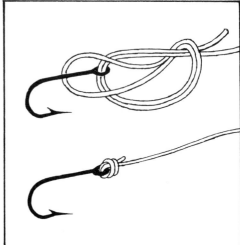

UNI KNOT
One of the strongest knots in use today. This is another good knot for connecting lead to a shock leader. It is also very popular among deep-sea anglers.

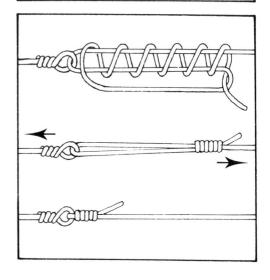

Knots

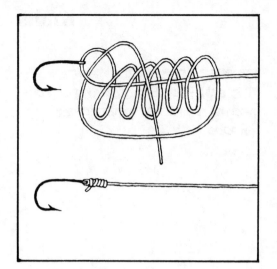

TUCKED HALF-BLOOD KNOT
For joining hooks, swivels and leads to line. Properly tied, this is a safe knot for joining a sinker to the end of a shock leader. Serious injuries have been inflicted by leads flying off during the cast. Frequently check the knot joining lead to leader.

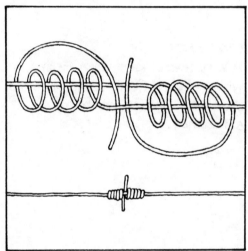

FULL BLOOD KNOT
The best knot for joining two lengths of line of the same, or similar, thickness.

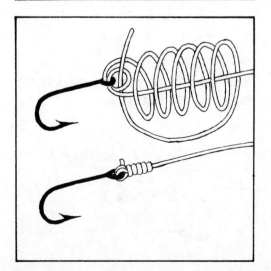

CLINCHED HALF-BLOOD KNOT
A better knot for use on heavier— gauged hooks.

Knots

DROPPER LOOP KNOT
The only knot for creating a connecting point for paternoster snoods.

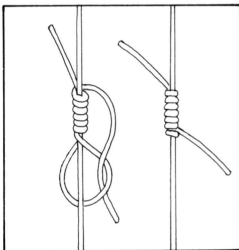

STOP KNOT
A very useful knot when fishing with a sliding float. Leave both tag ends very long for maximum efficiency.

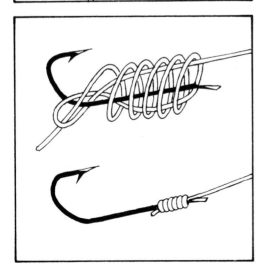

SPADE-END KNOT
Mainly used for making up a team of mackerel feathers.

Remember!

Salt water causes corrosion to metal surfaces. Reels and rod fittings both contain metal, and both items are expensive. After every fishing session, wash rod and reel under cold, fresh water.

Spray reels with water repellant, and oil and grease necessary points.

Every so often, strip reels down completely and clean the internal mechanism, re-grease and re-assemble.

By following this simple procedure your reel will last a lifetime and function efficiently to give you trouble-free fishing.

Index